Annie Dillard and R.S. Thomas have both suggested that the ability to see—to truly attend to something—is like a pearl of great price hidden in a field. That is to say, the power of attention is extraordinarily valuable and woefully difficult to find. This is why we need poets, artists, and writers in our lives skilled at the practice of focal attention. In this beautiful new volume from Matthew Dickerson and Matthew Clark, we have two friends training their eyes on the details of God's creation through printmaking, poetry, and theological reflection. There is plenty in these pages to inspire delight and wonder at the beauty of the earth. For my part, I'm also grateful for the treasure that is their ability to see it in the first place.

—**STEVEN PURCELL** executive director of Laity Lodge

Creation is ablaze with beauty, and this book helps us pay closer attention to astonishing creatures, landscapes, and watersheds, whether right outside our window or in a distant wilderness. Dickerson and Clark show how these encounters incite both praise and lament, provide rest and healing for our souls, and call for us to tend this wondrous yet wounded world.

—**WESLEY VANDER LUGT** author of *Beauty Is Oxygen: Finding a Faith that Breathes*

Over the shoulder, through the heart is always and everywhere the deepest learning. In *Birds in the Sky, Fish in the Sea,* Matthew Dickerson invites us to come and see the world that he knows and loves—the wilds of Alaska, the islands of California, the wetlands of Florida, and his own native New England with its forests, lakes, meadows and rivers, inch by slow inch opening the eyes of our hearts to cormorants and crows … to salmon leaping along the shoreline … to watermelon berries, huckleberries, blueberries, gooseberries, and thimbleberries … to the 350 varieties of crayfish … and yes, to the foraging black bear too. A wonderfully gifted professor who writes with unusual attentiveness about the whole of life and learning, this new book features the artful insight of Matthew Clark, whose artwork make this a beautifully-imagined window into the world, a meditative, poetic reflection that will be a good gift for all who long for eyes to see more and more and more.

—**STEVEN GARBER** author of *The Seamless Life: A Tapestry of Love and Learning, Worship and Work*

These words and pictures embody the pursuit at the heart of humanity's primordial vocation. The Edenic call to name the animals is more than mere taxonomy. Dickerson and Clark invite us to step beyond the reductive dissection of what a thing is, into that nobler posture of inquiry which wonders, "what does it mean?" In the leaves of this book we find our way back to the woods, where love for the world around us is essential to knowing it.

—**STEPHEN CROTTS** illustrator and hobby naturalist

BIRDS IN THE SKY
FISH IN THE SEA

MATTHEW DICKERSON
AND **MATTHEW L. CLARK**

BIRDS IN THE SKY
FISH IN THE SEA

ATTENDING TO CREATION WITH DELIGHT AND WONDER

SQUARE HALO
BOOKS

In Christian art, the square halo identified a living person presumed to be a saint. Square Halo Books is devoted to publishing works that present contextually sensitive biblical studies and practical instruction consistent with the Doctrines of the Reformation. The goal of Square Halo Books is to provide materials useful for encouraging and equipping the saints.

©2025 Square Halo Books, Inc.
P.O. Box 18954 | Baltimore, MD 21206
www.SquareHaloBooks.com

ISBN 978-1-941106-40-2
Library of Congress Control Number: 2024944372

Printed in the United States of America

In memory of
Willard W. Dickerson (1935–2024),
who took his eight-year-old son Matthew on his first
camping trip to Maine's Allagash Wilderness Waterway
and taught him the names of many of the birds whose
beautiful, mysterious, and delight-producing calls
we heard, including loons, American bitterns,
and common snipes.
—*Matthew Dickerson*

To my wife, Amy.
We've been together for every mile hiked,
swamp explored, rock flipped, canoe paddled, fossil dug,
and forest camped. She's loved me and encouraged me
to pursue my artwork with all my heart
since we were kids.
—*Matt Clark*

PRAISE THE LORD, YE CREEPING THINGS.

CONTENTS

Acknowledgements, Thanks, and Words of Gratitude

FROM MATTHEW DICKERSON

I thank my wife, Deborah, for many years spent faithfully partnering with me in marriage and parenting, for attentiveness to the corner of creation known as The Cobble where we make our home together (including Herculean efforts to remove invasive species), for regularly reminding me of the names and seasons of many of the wildflowers that blossom on the trails we walk together, and for encouraging—and helping me improve— my writing during our many years together. I am thankful also to my good friend David O'Hara for the many ways he has modeled such careful attentiveness to the world around us over the years we have known each other; I cherish our friendship. And thanks to my friends in the Chrysostom Society, past and present, who have formed such a wonderful community of faith and art and welcomed me into it; the many in our group who have already taken the big step toward our resurrected bodies and new creation are truly a great cloud of witnesses (Heb. 12:1).

Much of the final draft of this book was completed at
Ernest Gruening State Historic Park in Juneau while serving
with my daughter-in-law McKenna Dickerson as 2024
Artists-in-Residence for Alaska State Parks. I am thankful both
to Alaska State Parks and also to Middlebury College for making
that residency (and several earlier artist and writing residencies)
possible through faculty professional development funds.

Most of the poems that appear in this book were first
workshopped at Otter Creek Poets. Thanks to all of you poets
for offering your helpful and insightful comments, and especially
to David Weinstock for your leadership and vision. Among those
poems: "Agulukpak Morning" appeared in *Deep Wild,* 2023;
"Two Crows Sit" appeared in *The Mountain Troubador,* 2024.
"Kenning the Cobble" and "Cardinal at the Feeder in Winter"
were first published in *Forgotten Ground Regained: A Journal
of Alliterative Verse,* Issue 5, Winter, 2025.

FROM MATTHEW L. CLARK

The administration at The Geneva School, where I teach,
allows generous professional development time. I have periods
during the day to have fruitful conversations and meaningful time
to develop my artwork. I teach at a school that understands that
the faculty is the curriculum and for that curriculum to be of value,

its faculty need to hone their skills and develop their interests. Many of the prints and drawings in this book were made between classes and perhaps when I should have been lesson planning or grading tests. I am thankful to have such a great place to work.

I am also thankful for my students who ask so very many questions. They are curious about the wide world and they compel me to learn more and explore further.

Finally, I would like to express my love for my children, Abigail, Elias, Oliver, Asher, Isaiah, Eva and Annabelle. They have been on so many hikes, so many camping trips, fished so many bodies of water, and canoed so many miles with me that I cannot conceive of an outdoors without them. They all love creation as much as I do if not in exactly the same way that I do. And that is fitting, their love fills up what mine is lacking.

FROM THE TWO MATTHEWS

Most importantly we thank God, who created all the wonders of earth, sky, and water (including rivers and lakes as well as the seas); who created us with eyes to see and ears to hear (both physical and metaphorical), as well as nostrils to take in the scents and hands to feel the textures, and to be drawn through that wonder toward its Creator; and who gave us the meaningful work of caring for that creation.

Attentiveness as Worship

Over dinner at the 2024 Square Halo conference I described my book *Aslan's Breath* as a collection of artwork for which I had simply written the captions. My comment was intended partly in humor: I had written most of the book before seeing *any* of his work, while many of Ned Bustard's illustrations were inspired by passages from my book or by the scenes and characters I was writing about. Yet the comment was only half in jest. For many readers, Ned's beautiful linocut prints may be the best and most memorable part of the book. They are more than illustrations; they are works of art that stand on their own apart from my writing.

A few weeks later, Ned told me my comment had planted in his mind a seed for a collaboration between myself and Ned's friend and print-making mentor, Matthew Clark. Although Ned didn't yet have a fully-fledged idea of how it would all come together, he imagined a book written for readers who believed in a Creator and understood the universe to be the meaningful result of a loving act (not just the result of blind, purposeless chance), and who were drawn, by their belief in a Creator, to beauty: both the beauty of Creation (what many refer to as "nature") as well as the beauty brought into being through human minds and hands.

I was immediately excited by the idea. Although I had not met Matthew Clark, Ned and our mutual friend Tom Becker had introduced me to Matthew's work a few years earlier: his prints showed a careful attentiveness to creation around him, which both reflected and elicited a sense of wonder and delight. Attentiveness to creation is a trait I deeply value. My good friend (and frequent co-author) David O'Hara is one of the most creative, wise, and thoughtful persons I know. Not coincidentally, he is also one of the most attentive. His long practice of careful and loving attentiveness to creation has profoundly inspired me to be more attentive myself. Likewise, the nature writers whose works have most influenced me—authors including Wendell Berry, Annie Dillard, Robert Siegel, and Robin Wall Kimmerer—have done so through their attentiveness as well as through the elegance and beauty of their prose. So I began to imagine a book with attentiveness to creation as its core.

After Ned described to me his goals for the book, and how he imagined my text woven in and around the artwork of Matthew Clark, I suggested organizing the book around a few short essays about the spiritual value of attentiveness.

Though personal and narrative, these framing essays would be explicitly theological, with each suggesting some aspect of a biblical foundation for attentiveness to creation, thereby giving part of an answer to why Christians *ought* to be attentive to creation and what some of the benefits of such attentiveness are. Both Ned and Matthew liked the idea. And thus was this book born.

Each chapter begins with a short theological essay, followed by some creative works of narrative nonfiction prose and poetry drawing on my experiences of attentiveness, wonder, and delight, all interwoven with Matthew Clark's own artistic expressions of attentiveness, wonder, and delight. Though some of the essays were inspired by experiences in places known for awe-inspiring majestic beauty (like Katmai National Park and Preserve), others came from city parks and from our own backyards. Wilderness settings can be wonderful places to enjoy the beauty of creation (and I highly recommend visiting national parks for those who are able), but we don't have to be in the wild to learn to be attentive to, and delight in, the beauty God has made. For those who take the time to look, there is awe-inspiring beauty in a butterfly, a bumblebee, a dandelion, and even a blade of grass. (Remember in *The Lord of the Rings* when Éomer speaks of grass, and contrasts mere green earth with legends as though they had nothing in common? Aragorn replies, "The green earth, say you? That is a mighty matter of legend though you tread it under light of day!")

The point of this structure—and especially of the essays introducing each section—is to suggest that it is good to be drawn to beauty, and that there is more to our appreciation of creation than our own gratification: that attentiveness to creation is a meaningful spiritual act (or spiritual discipline) with several important benefits or goals; that God invites us to such attentiveness; and that to be attentive to creation as well as to the Creator—or, we might say, to be attentive to creation *as a way of* being attentive to the Creator—is an act of worship.

We hope this book leads its readers and viewers more deeply into delight, wonder, and ultimately into worship of our great Creator. It is a true collaboration between the author and the artist, inspired by the works of God who is both Author and Artist. Although some of our work emerged independently out of our individual experiences of delight and wonder at creation, my writing also drew directly on Matthew Clark's art, while some of his prints were inspired by my essays. Some of the book also grew out of time we spent together in Florida in May of 2024, and continued to grow in conversation.

—Matthew Dickerson
Summer 2024

Look at the Birds of the Air: Encountering the Creator through Creation

Look at the birds of the air. . . .
See how the flowers of the field grow.
—Matthew 6:26, 28

"Be still, and know that I am God," the sons of Korah tell us in Psalm 46:10. It is one of the best known and most often cited passages in the Psalms, and one so straightforward that translations ranging from the King James and Revised Standard to the New International, English Standard, and New Living Translation all render this Hebrew phrase with the same words in English. The second part of this command, "Know that I am God," is vitally important, of course. When God speaks through Moses to the Israelites in captivity to Egypt, he tells them, "I will take you as my own people, and I will be your God. *Then you will know that I am the Lord your God*" (Ex. 6:7, emphasis added). Hebrews 11:6 notes that belief in God's existence is the starting point of faith, and of pleasing God. But in Psalm 46, the psalmist suggests something interesting by preceding that instruction to know God with the imperative

"Be still." This first part of the command is also very important. Yet it seems much easier to ignore, especially in a culture that values and even idolizes busy-ness. The suggestion here is not that stillness is as important as knowledge of God, but rather that being still—what we might call a *practice* of stillness— is a starting point to knowing God. It is a *needed* step.

First we are still. Then we can know God.

To some, especially those who resist stillness, it may seem like too strong a point to call stillness a prerequisite to knowing God. But biblical faith requires more than mere intellectual knowledge; it requires what we might call a heart knowledge. Put another way, the goal isn't to know facts about God; the goal is to be in relationship with God himself. So we might wonder what this stillness looks like and how can it help us know God.

Looking at some other translations of this passage can give further insights. The New American Standard renders Psalm 46:10 as: "Stop striving, and know that I am God." Stillness, this translation suggests, is more than physical inactivity (though it may likely require that our bodies actually slow down); it is a letting go of our busy-ness and need to be doing things, or getting things done; it is a sort of quietness of mind and spirit. *The Message* translation opts for: "Attention, all! See the marvels of God!" This gets at the idea that stillness goes hand in hand with attentiveness. This, too, is helpful. To know God, we must pay attention to God. And to give our full and undivided attention to God, we need to lay down the many other things occupying us.

Being still, paying attention, and ceasing our striving are necessary for that heart knowledge of God. So we aren't able to follow the second command, to know God, unless and until we first take the time to be still. Without stillness, we cannot know God.

I wonder if there is something analogous going on—a similar combining of ideas—in the Sermon on the Mount when Jesus says:

> Look at the birds of the air; they do not sow or reap or store away in barns, and yet your heavenly Father feeds them. Are you not much more valuable than they? Can any one of you by worrying add a single hour to your life?
>
> And why do you worry about clothes? See how the flowers of the field grow. They do not labor or spin. Yet I tell you that not even Solomon in all his splendor was dressed like one of these. If that is how God clothes the grass of the

field, which is here today and tomorrow is thrown into the fire, will he not much more clothe you—you of little faith? So do not worry, saying, "What shall we eat?" or "What shall we drink?" or "What shall we wear?" (Matthew 6:26–31)

Consider the two illustrations from nature that Jesus uses in this teaching: "the birds of the air" and "the flowers of the field." One obvious conclusion from both examples is that we need not worry. Yet if we pay careful attention to this passage, we see that Jesus does more than give this moral teaching. In both examples, there is a three-part sequence: command, observation, rhetorical question. The first part is the command. In Jesus' first example, he commands his listeners to "look at the birds of the air." In his second example, he tells them: "See how the flowers of the field grow"— or as the King James poetically renders it, "Consider the lilies of the field." Jesus then moves from a command to an observation.

It is vain for you to eat the bread of sorrows.
for he giveth his beloved sleep.

The birds, he tells his listeners, "do not sow or reap or store away in barns, and yet your heavenly Father feeds them"; the flowers of the field, he says, "do not labor or spin. Yet I tell you that not even Solomon in all his splendor was dressed like one of these."

Finally, Jesus ends both illustrative examples with a spiritual lesson, which he gets across in both cases with a rhetorical question. After the first example, Jesus asks, "Can any one of you by worrying add a single hour to your life?" The answer, of course, is a resounding *No!* Indeed, modern science suggests that worrying has a negative impact on our bodily health and can take hours or even days or years away from our lives. The second rhetorical question is, "If that is how God clothes the grass of the field, which is here today and tomorrow is thrown into the fire, will he not much more clothe you—you of little faith?" Here, the obvious answer is *Yes! Yes, he will!* Consideration of the splendor with which God has arrayed the flowers of the field is supposed to make that answer clear. But just in case there are any questions, Jesus then explicitly states the command: "Do not worry."

So one lesson in this part of the sermon is that God loves us, watches out for us, and cares for us. Thus, we need not be anxious or afraid. We need not worry. This is a very important lesson. Considering all its variations, "Do not be afraid" is the most oft-repeated command in all Scripture. Yet I think we make a mistake if we jump too quickly to this spiritual *lesson* without taking time to obey the opening commands: *pay attention to the birds and flowers.* Jesus could have said, simply, "Do not be anxious." But he didn't. He told us to pay attention to the birds and the flowers. We ought not skip over this very important part of Jesus' sermon. Consider birds. Be attentive to flowers. Watch. Listen. Look. Smell. Be still. Missing out on the opening commands to pay attention to the birds and flowers is a bit like trying to know God without taking the time to be still. For one thing, abstract ideas like "do not worry" do not stick with us. We can give intellectual affirmation to the truth and importance of the principle, but that doesn't mean we remember it or follow the teaching. Taking time to meditate on God's created world—considering not only birds and flowers, but also fish and forests, meadows and mountains, lizards and Leviathan—helps shape our imaginations so that we become the sort of people who don't easily give into worry.

Indeed (and this is a second point) taking the time to consider creation is perhaps the most important way we can be still and know that God is God. It would be odd—we might even say hypocritical or dishonest—to have an acquaintance who was a composer, and to tell them that you were really interested in knowing them better, but then to spend no time listening to their compositions. Or to claim to want a deeper relationship with a friend who was a painter but never to take the time to look at their paintings.

So it is with God, the great Artist and Creator. If you want to know the Creator, be attentive to creation. David writes: "The heavens declare the glory of God; the skies proclaim the work of his hands. Day after day they pour forth speech; night after night they reveal knowledge" (Ps. 19:1–2). The Apostle Paul, in his letter to the Roman church, tells Christians that "God's invisible qualities—his eternal power and divine nature" can be "clearly seen … from what has been made" (Rom. 1:20). Both of these passages tell us that the work of God's hands— what we often call "nature" or "creation"— reveals knowledge about the Creator.

The insights we gain from attention to creation are many and varied. James, in his epistle, also invites his readers to pay attention to wildflowers not as an antidote to worry but in order to more deeply understand an important spiritual and moral principle about wealth and pride:

> But the rich should take pride in their humiliation—since they will pass away like a wild flower. For the sun rises with scorching heat and withers the plant; its blossom falls and its beauty is destroyed. In the same way, the rich will fade away even while they go about their business" (James 1:10–11).

After Job's three friends speak to him in ways God later describes as untrue, Elihu steps in and speaks words not unlike those Jesus would later speak in his Sermon on the Mount, telling Job to "stop and consider God's wonders" (Job 37:14). He goes on in more detail to call Job's attention to several of those wonders. The poet responsible for Psalm 104, rather than *instructing* people to be attentive to nature simply gives a long and wonderful *example* of attentiveness, writing about the numerous landscapes and creatures he has taken the time to ponder.

Considering the Bible as God's revelation given to us that we might know God better, it is worth noting that it begins in Genesis with a description of creation—*creation* both as a verb and a noun: both the creative activity of God and the results of that work. The text draws our attention to the stars, sun, and moon; to waters, plants, and trees; to living creatures in the water and the air and on the earth; and to wild animals as well as livestock. Indeed, the Spirit-inspired Word repeatedly invites us to reflect on the created world in order to come to know God. For example, Scripture points (in these passages and elsewhere) to the goodness, beauty, and majesty of creation in order to draw attention to God's own creative goodness and power. Psalm 104:24 epitomizes this theme well by turning observation of creation into praise of the Creator: "How many are your works, Lord! In wisdom you made them all; the earth is full of your creatures." Psalm 95:3–5 gets at a related idea, again inviting our reflection on creation in order to see the greatness of God:

> For the Lord is the great God, the great King above all gods. In his hand are the depths of the earth, and the mountain peaks belong to him. The sea is his, for he made it, and his hands formed the dry land.

Even the artwork in God's tabernacle (e.g., Ex. 25:34) and later in the temple (e.g., 1 Kings 6:18, 35) often draws from nature imagery to help priests and worshippers experience God's presence.

Benjamin Myers, in the introduction to his book *A Poetics of Orthodoxy,* draws an important and succinct conclusion:

> In his *Confessions,* Augustine tells how noticing the particular things of creation points us toward the creator God. Were we just to admire the object, of course, we would be in danger of idolatry. But when we allow our focused attention to point us through the object at the source of all being, then we have turned attention into prayer. . . . God speaks to us through beauty. Our attention to the particulars of the world—which is given in contemplation, in study, and in good art—honors God.

Yes. Being attentive to creation is a way not only to know God more fully, but even to honor God. The rest of this book is one practice in that attentiveness and our effort to do what Jesus instructed in the Sermon on the Mount, what Elihu told Job to do, and what various psalmists both practiced and announced as meaningful: to use our creative practices of both word and image to help us to pay attention and also to reflect on what we see.

KENNING THE COBBLE

I. Accidental Archway

Deborah called it   a magic door—
this white pine felled   by some fierce wind
across the trail   after roots and trunk
had drawn to itself   the earth's disease:
a leaning arch   leading away
from the vegetable garden   I vainly manage
toward the wild   wooded messiness
where we cling to no   conceit of control.

II. Vernal Visions

Bloodroot, spring beauty,   Dutchman's britches,
last autumn's leaves,   and trout lily,
festoon the forest   floor of springtime
gracing the ground   we tread together.
Coda pees and sniffs   piles of fresh pellets
dropped indiscreetly   by passing deer
who nibble buds   off berry bushes.
Here, too, hovers   the Holy Breath.

Revelation in the Backyard

For years, our black lab Coda joined us on walks around the
trails near our home. Like most dogs, he is attentive with his nose.
Good smells—which for a black lab means *any* smells, including
ones which to us are decidedly *not* good—always got him pulling
on his leash (and as a ninety-pound creature, he could pull
forcefully). When we let him off leash, he would bound through
the woods with exuberance. He was always the last one ready to
end the walk: when he sensed us turning toward home, he would
stubbornly dig in his heels, or he would flop down and roll over,
instantly ceasing our progress.

Admittedly, bringing him with us made our walks more
challenging, yet *his* need for those daily walks meant that we, too,
took walks. We had to be deliberate about it. Twice a day, one or
the other of us—and on the best days, both of us—would leash him
up and head out onto the trails meandering through the woods
either to the meadow, or the berry patch and clearing we call "deer
field," or in a wide loop below our house, or on rare occasions
when we felt especially ambitious up to the top of the hill.

Now, Coda is in the last stages of life. His rear hips are failing.
He wants to be with us wherever we are which often means
following us around the house, but he struggles on the stairs and
sometimes stumbles. As he has since his puppy days, he still likes
to play tug-of-war with me, but his mobility is limited and he
tires easily. Recent blood tests have suggested issues related to his
thyroid, and he has lumps on his belly. Even so, he still generally

gets excited when we tell him it is time for a walk. Though he now ambles along slowly at our sides rather than trying to bound away and is often ready to head home before we are, he is still attentive with his nose, noticing things that neither Deborah or I can see. Even under half a foot of snow, he can still find that pile of "milk duds" left behind by the passing deer, and if we aren't quick enough to pull back on his leash, he gets his quick treat.

To be honest, although I wrote "one or the other of us" would take him for a walk, my wife Deborah has walked Coda far more often than I have over his dozen-plus years with us. Although I am his favorite opponent in games of tug, I'm sure he prefers Deborah as a walking partner. For one thing, she is more patient with his side trips and sniffing. Maybe she appreciates his attentiveness more. Though she doesn't have Coda's nose, Deborah is also a wonderful model of attentiveness on her walks. She reports to me not only the number of whitetail doe flags that bound off through the woods, but also the number of little red efts she sees along the trails, how many little toads and wood frogs she spots, and which birds she sees or hears. She also knows the spring wildflowers that grow in the local woods and can guess within a week or two when each is likely to appear. She has not only learned their names, but she knows something about them both through her reading and her careful attentiveness to where and how they grow. When spring comes early she knows from the early appearance of the various vernal ephemerals.

A few of the wildflowers whose names she has told me have found a home in my memory. I'm especially fond of the spring ephemerals. Once you look closely at the delicate white shape of the Dutchman's britches, it's hard to forget their appropriately descriptive name—although I can't say they look much like the pants worn by my good friend of Dutch ancestry. I marvel that God made such a beautiful and intricately shaped blossom, and each spring when I see the first one pop up I have to bend over and admire it. We also have many red and white trillium around our house and especially on the north and east slopes of the hillside. With their large blossoms and bright colors, they really stand out in morning light. Their equally descriptive name, which means "three leaves," is also easy to remember.

The association of trout lilies with a fish I most enjoy catching makes it another easy-to-remember flower name for me. It is not their six-lobed yellow blossoms that I think of—since it takes

seven years for a trout lily to produce a single flower in order
to reproduce, I rarely even see the yellow blossoms—but their
green leaves with beautiful mottled red patterns reminiscent of
the coloration of various species of trout and char. The leaves are
sweet and tender, too, tasting better to me than even my favorite
garden greens. Yet because of the long slow process of the plants
maturing, I allow myself to nibble only a handful of leaves each
spring when I find an especially abundant patch.

Beyond these and one or two other flowers, however,
I frequently need Deborah to remind me of the names of
wildflowers we encounter on our walks. *Is that spring beauty or
hepatica?* I ask. She almost
always has the answer. It's
one reason I'm glad to
walk our woods with her.
Another is that she sees
things I miss, and that
helps me to see more.

Or at least to see differ-
ently. When I am walking
alone, my eyes are more
likely drawn up into the
canopy above, or farther out
in the forest, looking at big
things rather than down at
the little blossoms and red
efts. I'm usually looking at

trees in particular. One reason is practical: we have always heated our house at least partly with firewood from our hillside property. Since I don't cut down healthy trees for heat, I'm always making mental notes of where trees have fallen, or are standing dead, or are diseased or badly damaged. As I walk, I'm planning my winter or spring cutting to get to the trees before they rot on the ground.

Yet the deeper reason I pay attention to trees is that I love trees. I delight in them. They are a constant source of wonder. Even sitting inside the house looking out our windows from my favorite chair where I usually spend my morning prayer time, I often find myself gazing at the native trees in the woods around our house. The stand of eastern red cedar by the driveway through our south window draws numerous birds of a variety of species: chickadees, tufted titmice, nuthatches, blue jays, goldfinches, and, in the summers, our ruby-throated hummingbird. It is especially busy in the spring when birds flock to gather cedar berries, though through the thick branches and evergreen needles I often see only glimpses of numerous shapes fluttering from branch to branch.

The bark of the paper birch just outside our east-facing window catches the morning light beautifully in the sharp contrast between the thin, coal-black horizontal stripes and the white behind them. The sugar maple and black cherry provide a nice contrast to the birch, filtering and dappling the morning light through their foliage in the summer, and etching the sky during November stick season. The apple tree under the birch is another favorite bird roost in winter since it stands near our bird feeder. The nearest branches, where the cardinals often perch, are just a few feet from my window. I can see the scars where woodpeckers have been hammering at it.

Looking at these trees, my prayers often turn to praise for all their majestic beauty God has brought into being. I admire the varying colors of their barks and blossoms, the differences in nuts and fruits, and the shapes and coloration of their foliage in the spring as well as the fall. Even the shapes of their crowns and branches are distinct.

It was only when I moved to a house in the woods that I also began to learn more about trees and even to appreciate their varying fragrances. The strong wintergreen scent of the sweet black birch is my favorite, reminding me of the all-natural birch beer I drank as a teenager. If "fresh" has a smell, it is the smell of a sweet birch. Though it isn't the best wood for heating, when a storm takes down a mature sweet birch I try to get to it with my chainsaw so I can enjoy all that fragrance before it's gone. As I cut it up, I frequently pause and pick up a handful of sawdust and breath in the air. The eastern red cedars have a strong fragrance more woodsy than sweet, but still very pleasant. The deep red of their heartwood is not only beautiful but also has a resin which is naturally insect repellent; that color and resistance to moths makes it a wonderful wood for a sweater chest. Over the past two decades, so many of the cedars have died and fallen that I can now count on my fingers how many are left. I don't cut them down by choice, but when one falls in a storm,

I use the trunk for fence posts and sometimes cut a few large discs for my closet. And on the other end of the odor category, the wood of the native poplar trees along our driveway smells like urine. Many years ago I shared that bit of information with a Cub Scout troop as I led them on a tree-identification walk, and of course that was the one thing all the scouts remembered.

I also love not only the iconically smooth bark of beech trees, but also the way they hold on to green leaves long after the rest of the forest canopy has turned brown. On late October walks when the other trees have gone bare, I can spot the beech trees long before I get to them. And then there is the one large shagbark hickory just a few strides off our driveway, whose bark hangs in long loose tatters like a fraying garment. To recognize that the word "bark" applies both to the smooth skin of the beech and the giant flaking scales of the shagbark hickory is as glorious as recognizing that a Saint Bernard and a chihuahua are both dogs.

Then there are the sugar maples in autumn when they flame in shades of red, orange, and yellow and their fallen leaves are worthy of hanging in the finest museums. I often stop and pick up some of the best ones just to strew across my desk or dining room table. It's hard to imagine that a tree painted with such artistic beauty in the fall can also produce in March the sweet sap that boils down to the finest syrup that makes our pancakes, oatmeal, and even my coffee so much tastier. And in late April, the three red maples in our yard blossom in tight clusters of red and yellow, and hungry pollinators looking for food in the early spring swarm to their branches. I can see why psalmists reference trees so often, using them as metaphors (Psalm 1), praising God for their majesty (Psalm 104), or imagining the mystery of how trees, too, join in the creation-wide glory of praising their—and our—Creator (Psalm 148).

The hill by our house is known as The Cobble: a proper noun that is also a common noun that in the northeast United States simply means "a rounded hill." So, like Bilbo Baggins who lives on a hill called The Hill, I live on a cobble called The Cobble. Our cobble rises about four hundred feet above our driveway. It is an outcropping of calcium-rich rock known as Dunham Dolostone, apparently from when our valley was at the bottom of an ocean and for eons collected the sediment of the shells and bones of sea creatures. It is similar in composition to the marble quarried a few miles from our home and crushed for its calcium carbonate. As a result of the rich acid-neutralizing soil, we have a wide variety of tree species, some of which are able to live at the edges of their ranges. In addition to the sugar maple and sweet (black) birch which dominate much of the hillside along with silvery smooth-skinned beech, paper birch, and a scattering of aromatic

red cedar around the yard, we also find American hophornbeam (which, unlike oak and beech, bear fruit every year, making them important to wildlife such as deer and turkey), a few red maple, a variety of soft maple, black cherry, white cedar, a few oak, poplar, shagbark hickory, pignut hickory, ash, hemlock, fir, a scattering of yellow birch, and large numbers of eastern white pine which dominate a grove south and west of our house. We refer to that grove as Narnia because of the sense of quiet there on our winter morning walks.

One of the delights of caring for many acres of woodland is that I occasionally get to walk the woods with professional foresters and trained botanists. The more I learn about the forest, the more I appreciate it and the more attuned I become to particular details as I walk. Each little part of the forest—with its unique mix of plant communities, soil types, vernal springs, and amount of daylight—seems to attract different mixes of creatures, all of which have adapted for millennia to different conditions. Only recently I have begun to learn how different species of moths and caterpillars (collectively known as *Lepidoptera*) in their larval (caterpillar) stages are able to feed only on very specific plants. Caterpillars of monarch butterflies, for example, are famously able to feed only on species of milkweed. I have also learned that while our woodland birds have varied diets as adults that may include seeds, insects, fruit, or a combination of these, many species are dependent on moth caterpillars to feed their chicks. The soft-bodied caterpillars are the only things the parents can squish down the little throats, so the birds need the insects which are dependent not just on trees and flowers in general, but on species-specific varieties of plants. Now, when I brush mow our small meadow in a little bowl between two wooded hills, I am careful to leave standing as much of the milkweed as I can. After I mow, the meadow looks like a teenager's messy room—or like the face of somebody shaving with a razor that has big gaps in it. When my walks through the woods take me through the meadow, I pay attention to what I find dining on that milkweed.

Unlike the author of Psalm 1, or even Jesus who drew spiritual lessons from the birds of the air and lilies of the field, I generally don't look for explicit spiritual messages when I sit and observe creation. I am willing just to find delight and wonder, and to turn that into praise. An attempt to turn attentiveness into a "lesson" or "moral" often feels forced to me, and in a way devalues the

goodness of the creation itself. It is not unlike churches that, unable to appreciate the artistic value of a painting or photograph, feel the need to add an inspirational message to the image in order to legitimize it or spiritualize it. And yet … pondering the amazing interconnectivity of plants, insects, birds, and trees in the little bit of land around our home, I think there is something in that bit of creation that really is reflecting the character of the Creator—something more than (or different from) the importance of the beauty itself. One of the common New Testament metaphors for the church is a body, and Paul writes how the body is made of many different parts with different purposes and characteristics, and yet all the parts are interdependent. When each part is healthy and functions according to its purpose, the body thrives. When one part suffers, the entire body suffers. One of the phrases in Robin Wall Kimmerer's beautiful book *Braiding Sweetgrass* that stuck with me was "all flourishing is mutual." Paying attention to our yard, and to our efforts to honor God's plan in how we care for our yard, we can see both the interconnectedness of the parts, and also the principle of mutual flourishing. Indeed, I think ecology in general points us to that principle.

I also find that we delight in those forests more because of our knowledge. As I wrote that sentence, I pondered whether it is because we love the land that we seek to be attentive and know it, or because we pay attention to it that we have come to love it more. The answer, I think, is both. Or maybe it's even more accurate to say that we both love the land and seek to be attentive to it because we love the Creator who made it.

Cardinal at the Feeder in Winter

The cardinals arrive first, as a couple,
shortly after the snow stops
falling. The female with her faded orange
beak stays back, perched on a branch

of a young apple tree in the yard where
a hairy woodpecker has knocked holes
in the bark. The bolder male moves in
closer despite sudden unwanted company:

a wild flurry of chickadee wings,
and pushy tufted titmice who prefer
their feast foraged straight from the feeder.
The larger cardinal likes his sunflower

seeds scattered across on the ground
where his scarlet cape stands out
against the white. My wife obliges,
always spreading extra seed

wishing for a glimpse of those wings
spread like a swath of blood on snow.
Snow which covers—like love,
or like mulch in spring—a multitude of sins.

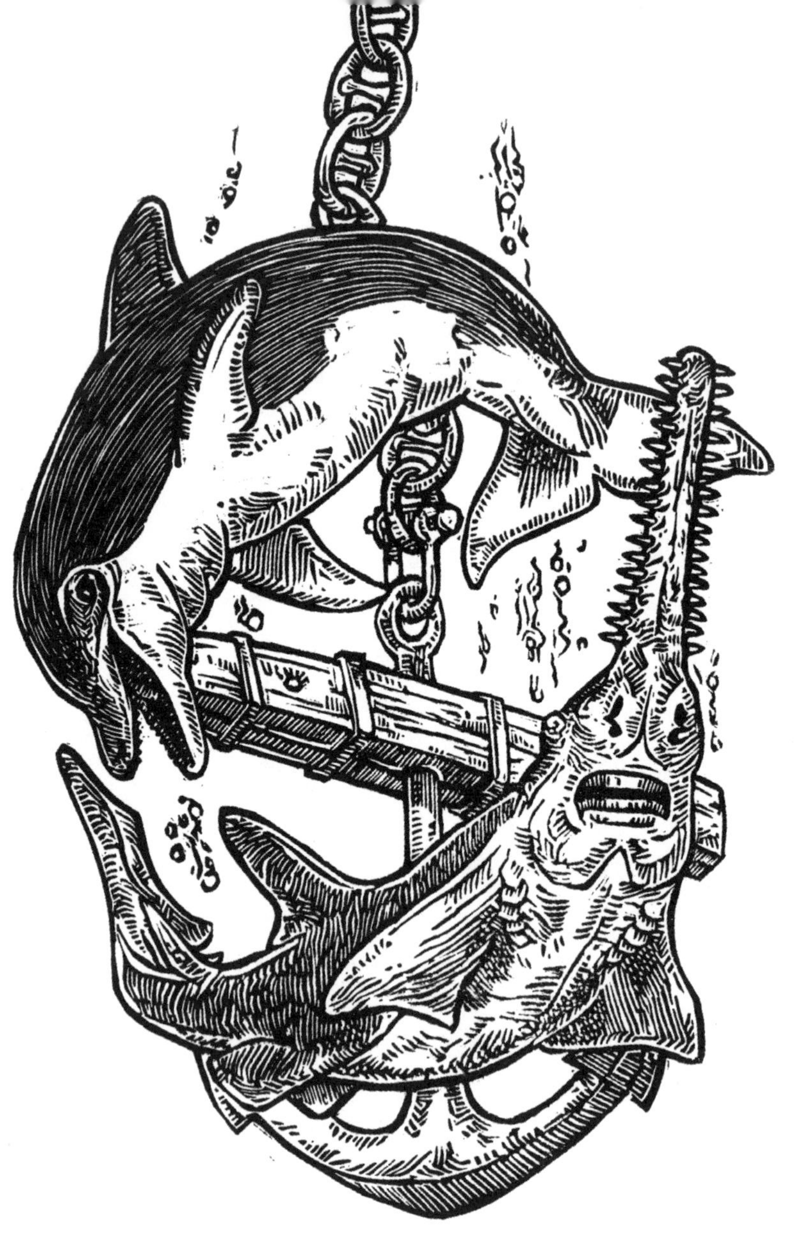

Which He Formed
to Frolic There:
The Value of Awe,
Wonder, and Delight

When I began working on this book and thinking about attentiveness, one of the first topics that came to mind was the spiritual value of wonder and delight. In a *Christianity Today* article titled "A Midnight Clear" (December 2023), Cory Gatliff argues for the importance of awe and wonder by drawing on several biblical passages that reference stars. "For Christians," the pastor notes, "awe leads to wonder, which leads to worship. Awe has a decentering effect that directs our attention away from the self, which is no small thing in a world awash with algorithms that cater to our every preference." Christians, I think, should see worth in anything that turns our attention away from a self-focus. Gatliff's biblical exploration points out more deeply that awe and wonder are themselves a good thing.

Much of his article focuses on the value of pondering stars and nighttime skies, or more generally what we often refer to as "the heavens," in order to elicit wonder. We see this most famously in Psalm 19 in which David writes about many ways that the heavens declare God's glory. But the idea appears many other places as well. Psalm 8 speaks of the glory God has set in the heavens. Psalm 33:6 speaks of God making the starry hosts by the breath of his mouth. And this is a reminder of the Genesis 1 creation account—our first revelation of God's character, nature, and power—in which the skies and the stars are among the first aspects of creation we read about. Not surprisingly, therefore, we read in Genesis 15:5 of God calling Abraham outside and telling him, "Look up at the sky and count the stars."

In Isaiah 40:26, God's prophet exhorts the people:

Lift up your eyes and look to the heavens:
Who created all these?
He who brings out the starry host one by one
and calls forth each of them by name.
Because of his great power and mighty strength,
not one of them is missing.

Commenting on this passage, Gatliff points out a "dynamic" played out in which "God instructs his people to look toward the heavens. Then awe excites wonder: 'Who created all these?' The wonder culminates in worship, as we contemplate 'he who brings out the starry host one by one and calls forth each of them by name.'"

In Isaiah 29:14, God makes an interesting promise regarding his wayward people: "Therefore once more I will astound these people with wonder upon wonder." The premise of the message spoken through Isaiah is important: in order call his people back to himself, God promises to fill them with wonder. Not just wonder, but *wonder upon wonder*. The implication is that when God's works elicit wonder, they point us back to God. Or at least they can when we pay attention—when we allow ourselves to experience wonder in response to God's wonders. Perhaps that is why Elihu speaks with awe of God's works in creation, repeatedly calling on Job to consider the skies or the heavens (Job 35:5, 36:28–33, 37:15–18). Elihu's discourse includes the exhortation to "Remember to extol [God's] work which people have praised in song" (36:24) and includes such exclamations of praise as, "How great is God—beyond our understanding" (36:26). Elihu punctuates the passage with the instruction we referenced in the previous section: "Listen to this, Job: stop and consider

God's wonders" (37:14). This is phrased as an imperative, like "be still" or "consider the lilies," which tells us not only that finding wonder at God's works is a good thing, but also that taking the time to "stop and consider" is an act of obedience that requires effort. While a sense of wonder can be thought of as a feeling that arises in response to something, for us to experience wonder we must choose to stop and be attentive—as Jesus instructed his followers to do with the birds and flowers. Indeed, the "wonders" Elihu refers to are not human feelings at all but acts of God; the *wonder* we feel comes as a response to being attentive to the *wonders* God creates. Pondering again the words of Jesus and Elihu, I would venture to say that wonder is a virtue that we practice and develop: a spiritual discipline we are told to exercise.

We could go on. The author of Proverbs also points to the majesty of the heavens in trying to communicate the wisdom of God: "By wisdom the Lord laid the earth's foundations, by understanding he set the heavens in place; by his knowledge the watery depths were divided, and the clouds let drop the dew" (Prov. 3:19-20).

As I ponder these biblical passages, it seems to me that followers of Christ ought to have, or ought to develop, a sense of wonder, and also that attentiveness to the works of God— including his great and ongoing work of creation—is one of the things that can open us up to the wonders God has made. In the opening chapter, I cited Psalm 95:3–5: "For the Lord is the great God, the great King above all gods. In his hand are the depths of the earth, and the mountain peaks belong to him. The sea is his, for he made it, and his hands formed the dry land." The psalmist seems to be drawing specifically on a sense of wonder at creation in order to communicate God's greatness, reminding us to consider two particularly awe-inspiring works of God: the towering mountain peaks and the vast and wild seas. Although I hope this book makes it clear that God's wonders can also be seen in a tiny mason bee landing on a marigold in our backyard, or in a little cloudberry growing in a bog, and that we ought to be attentive to the small creations of God as well as the larger and more majestic ones, for the psalmist to point to mountains and seas would certainly elicit wonder.

Indeed, though in his essay Gatliff focuses on stars, he points out there are many aspects of creation that can lead to the awe and wonder and thus to worship: "Standing on the rim of the Grand Canyon; being surrounded by towering mountains; or experiencing more intimate moments, like holding a newborn or sitting in the presence of a loved one close to death." As a lover of rivers, I appreciate the author of Psalm 98 who, in eliciting our sense of wonder and then turning that wonder to praise and awe of God as righteous judge, includes rivers along with seas and mountains as aspects of creation that point us toward God as they join in creation-wide worship:

Let the sea resound, and everything in it, the world, and all who live in it. Let the rivers clap their hands, let the mountains sing together for joy; let them sing before the Lord, for he comes to judge the earth. He will judge the world in righteousness and the peoples with equity (Psalm 98:7–9).

I write this paragraph just three days after a visit with my wife to Glacier Bay National Park in Alaska, where we gazed up at a glacier a mile wide—with a front face three hundred feet high—calving into the ocean. In the background stood a mountain range that rose from sea level to a peak over fifteen thousand feet in elevation. We saw humpback whales breaching, orcas hunting in the shallows, islands covered with roaring sea lions, a huge brown bear grazing on berries along the sides of a steep bluff, and a colony of seabirds beyond count that included puffins, gulls, kittiwakes, and cormorants all living in community. Any one of those alone was enough to produce in me an overflow of awe and wonder. And even as my eyes were often drawn upward, our friend Nina, who was with us on the trip, continued to experience wonder at the delicate grasses, leaves, ferns, mosses, and blossoms growing along the edges of marshes and bogs near the shoreline of Glacier Bay.

Everything I just wrote about wonder could be said as well about delight—which is similar to wonder and often goes hand in hand with it. To see the value of delight, consider first that it is very different from greed, and may even be its opposite. Greed seeks to possess and control. Delight, by contrasts, finds joy in the thing itself and is thus much more like love. Delight takes pleasure in the goodness of creation, which leads to a recognition of the goodness of the Creator, which (for Christians) in turn leads to worship of that Creator.

One of the things that has always struck me about Psalm 104—which I referenced earlier as a biblical example of attentiveness to creation, practiced through the art of poetry—is how the unnamed psalmist finds delight, wonder, and awe in creation, and in doing so worships the Creator. My favorite verses of this psalm are 25–26, which not only praise God for creating a "sea, vast and spacious" and for creating the "creatures beyond number … both large and small" which dwell there, but specifically for forming the Leviathan to frolic there. The psalmist seems to take particular joy in the thought of the Leviathan frolicking. My pastor, Dr. Allen, who holds a doctorate focused on ancient semitic languages, including biblical Hebrew told me about the verb used in this passage that is often translated to "frolic." The lectionary definition gives three meanings: "to make sport," "to jest," and "to play (including instrumental music, singing, dancing)." Although each of these definitions has a different meaning, they all carry the sense of *doing something whose main purpose is not work related or done for productivity*: the activities do not put food on the plate or income in our pockets; they don't lead in any *direct* way to our survival. All of them are activities done for the sake of delight.

We see similar ideas throughout Psalm 104. In addition to praising God for that which is useful such as cattle, oil, wine, and bread, the psalmist takes note of aspects of creation that (like frolicking) have no particular usefulness to humankind in an agrarian society such as that of ancient Israel. In addition to the Leviathan, the psalm mentions wild donkeys, birds of the sky, storks, wild goats, the hyrax (whatever that is), and the prowling beasts of the forest. The psalm repeatedly praises God for providing for all of these creatures. In another expression of delight and wonder (and another example of paying attention especially to birds) the psalmist also mentions how "birds of the sky … sing among the branches." I am also appreciative of this! In the summer when our windows are open, my wife and I love to wake at dawn to the sounds of the wood thrush, hermit thrush, gray catbirds, robins, veeries, red-eyed vireos, and a variety of warblers singing in the trees beside our Vermont house. (Although there are times I could do without the male cardinal who scolds and sometimes physically attacks his reflection in our windows.)

But what is perhaps most remarkable for a psalmist coming out of an agrarian culture in which sheep played a vital role— a psalmist some have conjectured might have been David himself, a former shepherd boy—is that the psalmist praises God for providing food for the lions, which would have been a natural enemy of a shepherd. In *Reflections on the Psalms,* C.S. Lewis observes that the Jews (unlike the contemporary Greeks) were a monotheistic culture with a strong Creator-creation story. He then notes, "What [the Jews] do give us, far more sensuously and delightedly than anything I have seen in Greek, is the very feel of weather—weather seen with a real countryman's eyes, enjoyed almost as a vegetable might be supposed to enjoy it." In his own stories, Lewis did a wonderful job communicating joy, delight, and wonder in creation, including the weather. I suspect this is one reason why his works found such a widespread following even among those who don't share his theistic faith. The same could be said of J.R.R. Tolkien, who was not only Lewis's close friend but an important influence on his journey to Christian faith. Those familiar with Middle-earth legends only through the film adaptations may think of the stories in terms of battles and action adventure, but careful readers of *The Hobbit* and *The Lord of the Rings* will remember that the author devoted many more pages to describing meals, flowers, trees, and landscapes, all with wonderfully descriptive details full of delight. *The Hobbit,* especially, is full of descriptions of meals.

And while on the subject of meals, consider the act of eating, and the variety of flavors, colors, and textures of the foods. God made the world that way: to bring delight to his creatures through their senses, including through the beauty we see and the flavors we taste! Thus in Psalm 34:8, David exhorts his listeners to "taste and

see that the Lord is good." Although I'm sure there are important metaphorical meanings to this exhortation, the literal meaning should not be ignored: look at the beauty of creation, and enjoy the goodness of food, and in doing so delight in the Lord and recognize his goodness. Genesis 3:6, although it comes in the middle of the story of the disobedience of the man and woman, reveals that the fruit God made in the garden was both "good for food and pleasing to the eye." Although eating the fruit of this one *particular* tree was an act of disobedience, the context reveals that the woman had already experienced the goodness and beauty of food in the fruit God had given them to eat, and thus she already knew how to recognize these qualities—qualities we can enjoy independent of the nutritional value of the food necessary to sustain our biological lives. God had created us in a way to delight in beauty and in our physical senses, and created a world that would satisfy that delight.

Wonder and delight are also childlike attributes. Maybe that's why many adults no longer allow themselves to experience the wonder of creation: they consider such a response of wonder to be *un*-adult. Most children aren't ashamed to get excited by an ant crawling along the ground, or a bumblebee burrowing into a large blossom. Walking around the yard or the woods with my three-year-old grandson reminds me of this. Each little raspberry blossom, maple leaf, or swallowtail butterfly is an opportunity for him to stop and watch and exclaim that sense of wonder and delight. When Matt Clark and I first began collaborating on this book, I toured the Orlando Wetlands with him and the younger children in his family, and later in the day we visited a small city park near his house. The kids were at times more attentive than I, pointing out spawning fish, finding the giant tortoise eating grass, and even spotting the big snapping turtle hiding near the stream bottom, always filled with delight and wonder. I'm reminded of Jesus' words, "Truly I tell you, unless you change and become like little children, you will never enter the kingdom of heaven. Therefore, whoever takes the lowly position of this child is the greatest in the kingdom of heaven" (Matt. 18:3–4). Jesus does not explicitly state which childlike qualities he is thinking of, though the word "lowly" suggests that humility is part of it. Many have suggested that it's childlike faith we need, and I don't doubt that. But when I think of childlike attributes, wonder and delight also come to mind.

Two Crows Sit

On the highest branch
of a pine, long dead,
its wood worn and bleached
almost white, catching
the morning sunlight
with a shine
that almost matches
the radiance
of their black wings.

FEASTING ON SALMON IN KATMAI NATIONAL PARK

It's a hot day in early August—hot, that is, by the standards of a tundra landscape in Alaska's Katmai National Park and Preserve. I'm standing on the rim of a gorge with several college students and a guide, the flat windy plain behind us, looking down into a gravelly river bottom dotted with brush and alders. Below us, thousands of sockeye salmon are migrating upriver to spawn. Seen up close, they are beautiful to behold: olive-green heads separated by curving paint-by-numbers lines; their crimson bodies blur into bright orange tails, and their bellies are painted in mottled blue and purple that spill up their sides like flames. The females are streamlined like trout, but the males sport awkward humps on their backs and toothy hooked noses (or upper lips) called kypes that give a ferocious quality to their beauty.

Two weeks ago, when they still swam out in the ocean, the salmon didn't look like they do now; they still had silvery sides and to the untrained eye appeared similar in shape and color to the other four species of Pacific salmon that spawn in Alaskan rivers. But once the sockeye salmon entered fresh water to spawn, they began to undergo their final transformations, taking on their distinctive shape and coloration. They will spawn and then they will die.

Or, rather, all of them will die, but only some will spawn— many will not make it that far. Even those that have escaped seals, sea lions, porpoises, and orcas, as well as the purse seines and longlines of commercial fisheries, still face a gauntlet of brown bears and other creatures looking for an easy meal along

much of the length of what can be a very long journey. On the
Yukon River, Chinook salmon travel more than two thousand
miles across the heart of Alaska and deep into Canada to spawn
on their natal streams, which they are able to find with nearly
miraculous accuracy matching any GPS navigation system. That
alone is a fact worthy of wonder. Even in the Lower 48, there are
runs of both Chinook and sockeye salmon over nine hundred
miles long up the Columbia River to the Snake River and into the
Salmon River and its tributaries deep into Idaho.

The sockeye salmon I am looking at have come only about
a hundred miles from the ocean, gaining twelve hundred feet in
elevation in the process—a relatively short spawning run, though
still quite impressive. They are so thick in some of the pools
and deeper channels around the river bends below me that for
stretches a hundred yards long and thirty yards wide I cannot
see the gravel river bottom. The river appears
to be stained dark red, as though a
local paint company had
a catastrophic
spill.

But while the sockeye stand out as both the brightest and most numerous fish in the river, they are not the only colorful creatures swimming around. Nor even, to my eye, the most beautiful. That honor I bestow upon the Dolly Varden char, which are in the river chasing the spawning sockeye. Although later in the year when food grows more scarce, Dollies will begin to feast on the plentiful dead salmon flesh floating downstream, their focus now is on the abundance of eggs that never find their way down into the safety of the gravel river bottom to hatch but instead float down the current by the millions, like small pink pearls or tapioca bubbles in bubble tea, except with a lot more protein. The Dollies are gorging on these. A small Dolly spending its entire life in a small mountain stream (or even a larger one that has just come into the river, fresh from a sojourn in saltwater) has a subtle beauty, with pale silvery green sides and decorative magenta dots densely scattered from their gills back to their tails. But a big male Dolly Varden approaching

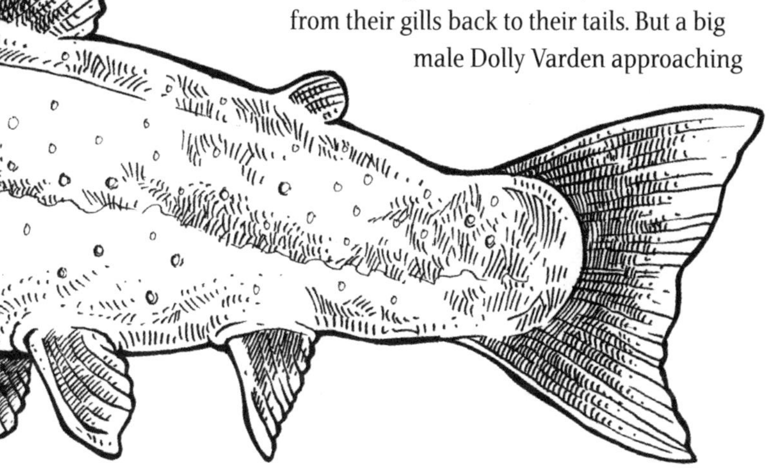

its own spawning season, that has swum
upriver out of some deep lake to follow the
migrating salmon, is more ostentatious,
with an orange underbelly and fin tips,
brilliant orange-and-yellow lips that
look like they've been applied with glossy
lipstick, and sides so bright green they
might make an emerald jealous. Leaping
from that green are spots ranging in shade from
magenta to a blood-red that rivals even the sockeye
they are chasing. The Dollies will find a pool just
downstream of a gravelly riffle where sockeye are
actively spawning, or perhaps just a little depression
only a few inches deep right behind a female laying
her eggs, and hold there gorging on the rich feast
floating over them.

Most of the world around them is doing the same
thing. Rainbow trout, whose evocative name suggests their own
colorful beauty, share the river with the Dolly Varden char often
competing with them for the prime feeding grounds—although
the river is so full of salmon and their eggs that competition
isn't always needed. Where rivers and streams empty into a
near alpine lake, Arctic char and lake trout (another species
of char) can also be found gobbling up drifting salmon eggs.
In numerous other Bristol Bay rivers, I've also found Arctic
grayling gorging on salmon eggs alongside the trout and char.
And though at first their drab olive coloration may make their

beauty more subtle, they, too, or a stunningly gorgeous fish. Their outsized dorsal fins create a wondrous profile, resembling ocean-going sailfish more than any freshwater fish I've ever seen. What appears at first as olive sides turns out to disguise scales that can be range from powder blue to shades of purple, decorated by patterns of black flecks. And their fins—both dorsal and adipose—can be fringed in red or veined like river rocks with myriad bright colors and hues. Eagles, seagulls, foxes, and wolves, also join in the feasting, eating the remains of fish that find themselves on the shore. And then there are the brown bears. Their livelihood in this Alaskan landscape—a landscape simultaneously harsh and abundant, fragile and resilient—depends on this annual protein-rich feast of ocean-born nutrients that makes its way upriver in the form of salmon and their eggs. They have only a few months each year to put on the hundreds of pounds of fat necessary to sustain them through winter. When the salmon are abundant, and the catching is relatively easy, the bears don't even bother eating the salmon flesh; they focus on the eggs. On this day, the air that feels hot even to me is especially hot to a 650-pound animal wearing a permanent fur coat. So after a morning feasting on sockeye, the brown bear sow has led her three spring cubs up out of the canyon into a shady gully where they can cool off and rest

on a remnant snowpack.
Mama sprawls out on the snow
to nap. Two of her cubs follow
her example. But one of the
cubs is not ready to nap—
it's pestering its sibling.
Soon, two of them
are rolling together
on the snow,
wrestling and
playing

bear-cub
games.
The cubs are
little furballs of fun.
I would love to go down and pet
one or join in the games like I do with
my black lab at home who is always up
for playing "tug" with a rope or one of his stuffed animals. But with
a six-hundred-pound sow keeping guard from a few yards away,

I suspect such an attempt would be the last thing I ever did. I will have to wait for the day in the new kingdom when the wolf lives with the lamb, the leopard lies down with the goat, the calf is safe with the lion, and brown bear sow allows humans to pet her cubs. So we watch from a safe distance atop the nearby bluff.

As I ponder the scene with joy, delight, fascination, and a little bit of longing, it is impossible for me *not* to see the activity below me as play. Some biologists might point out that the cubs' activities can be explained merely as training for the rough-and-tumble world they will grow into as adults, and that to refer to it as "play" is a form of anthropomorphizing: imagining a human trait that isn't really there in the thoughts and behavior of bears. On the one hand, they are correct that adult bears must compete physically with one another for the rights to prime hunting spots on the salmon streams and berry patches. On more than one occasion, I've watched these battles near rivers. Competition among males to mate can lead to even more intense combat. And since females normally nurse their young for two to three years, during which time they are not estrous, male brown bears will eat even their own cubs in order to get the females ready to mate again. Females need to be constantly vigilant, and will aggressively chase off even much larger males that come near their young in order to defend them. It's a life-and-death matter. Does the seemingly playful swatting, biting, rolling, and wrestling of the young cubs prepare them for a harsh life when they're no longer under their mother's protection? I have no doubt it does. It can be a matter of life and death for them.

Yet I still sit and delight in the playfulness of these cubs. And I write this paragraph just a few days after watching large pods of both common dolphins and bottlenose dolphins surfing the wakes of our tour boat as we crossed the Santa Barbara Channel to Channel Islands National Park. They repeatedly leapt high in the air all around us and at times got as close to the bow of the boat as possible, racing alongside us while weaving in and around each other. My wife and I watched this scene of play with a joy and delight that brought us to tears. I have also seen videos of crows repeatedly tumbling head-over-wings in an updraft of air only to fly back to their starting place and do it again, and of otters sliding down snowbanks and then climbing back up to do it again.

All of these seemingly playful activities—of bear, dolphin, crow, otter, and many other creatures as well—consume precious calories in a world in which survival is not taken for granted, and yet they do not in any *direct* way contribute to the biological necessities of reproduction or acquiring food. So while some biologists may critique the use of the word "play" to describe these activities, other experts in animal behavior have pointed out the human arrogance of thinking we have a monopoly on "play" and argued that playfulness is indeed a property of many intelligent creatures.

That latter opinion is not only something I have observed in nature, but it also seems to be the perspective of the Bible. In calling the naptime distractions of these bear cubs "play," I take to heart the words of the psalmist who wrote of the frolicking Leviathan. Yes. God made creatures to frolic! He put playfulness into their hearts, even as he put it into our human hearts. What the psalmist said of Leviathan surely is true of the bear cub, the kitten, and the dog—not only the puppy, but the full-grown canine. We can see it also in the crow, the dolphin, the otter. There is delight in play. And maybe even something deeper: something in the very nature of the type of delight that comes from play. In many ways, frolic is also fundamentally incarnational. The play of these animals is done with physical bodies, and with the material substance of creation. God created the physical world and he made our physical bodies. He made it all good, even as both work and rest are good. God made us to play and to delight, even as he made us for joy and wonder. This is evident in creation. Surely delight is good for me also. Surely it reflects something in the nature of the God that we worship who fashioned all creation. Including the Leviathan. Including the bear cubs. We worship a God who delights in play, and who made a universe where work is balanced not only by rest, but by the need to frolic.

Deep Calling

The water has pulled away from the shore,
receding into the darker green of the deep
exposing rocks like bleached bones where
gulls pick at flesh of mussels and clams,
emptying the shells to be ground to sand.

Yet to these bones the periwinkles cling.
Crabs walk in weeds, hide in pools left
by the ebbing tide—harbors also for
tiny krill almost too small to see,
for baby mackerel striped blue and black.

Puffins venture close to shore to mate.
They fill nests with eggs on islands of rock.
Newborns chicks will swim out to sea
like the fleeing tide, into that unknown.
They will not see land for many years.

Restoring the Soul: Creation, Rest, and Quiet

The Lord is my shepherd, I lack nothing.
He makes me lie down in green pastures,
he leads me beside quiet waters,
he refreshes my soul.
—Psalm 23:1–3

Theologically speaking, we all need rest. And I'm not talking about sleep—though that, too, is important.

Consider again the teachings of Jesus in the Sermon on the Mount. It was as an antidote to worry or anxiety that Jesus called his disciples to consider the birds and lilies. When our souls are *not* at rest is when we especially need to be led to green pastures, and to pay attention to the birds and flowers. Or consider Jesus' own example: in the busiest times of his ministry, when he needed restoration himself, he made a point of frequently withdrawing to lonely places to pray (Mark 1:35, Luke 5:16). Genesis 3:8 suggests that it was in the garden in the cool of the day that Adam and Eve were used to meeting with God before their sin made them afraid of him.

In Psalm 65, David refers to God as "the hope of all the ends of the earth," and praises him, saying "[You] formed the mountains by your power" (5–6). The psalm, with its reference to the mountains and the seas, goes on to speak of the whole earth as being filled with awe at God's wonders. We could have considered this psalm in the previous chapter as an example of awe and wonder at creation (especially at the mountains and seas) leading to praise. Yet there is something else in this passage as well, for David goes on to mention God's strength in having "stilled the roaring of the seas, the roaring of their waves, and the turmoil of the nations" (7).

This nature-imagery points to God bringing about peace and rest—in the words of the psalmist, stillness—in the midst of turmoil and chaos. It is in immediate response to God calming the seas that David goes on to speak of God's wonders, saying that such wonders have "call[ed] forth songs of joy" (8). He goes on speak of "grasslands of the wilderness" overflowing and the hills being "clothed in gladness." As he so often does in his poetry, David points us to nature as a way of pointing us toward God, and in this case specifically pointing in the direction of peace, rest, and stillness.

Consider also the vision of the new Jerusalem and the new heaven and new earth that John passes on to the church in Revelation 21–22. Scripture also uses the imagery of cities to point to God's kingdom, in addition to the nature imagery we have focused on in this book. The overall image of God's new kingdom in a restored creation is of a glorious new city. Revelation contains more than two dozen references to cities, and while some (especially in Revelation 18) are to the city of Babylon which is destined for destruction, many are to the Holy City, the New Jerusalem. Exploring that imagery would require another book entirely (and others have written such books). My own thought is that in times in which both the Book of Psalms and the New Testament were written, cities provided both safety and community; they were where the synagogues were found and where one didn't have to worry about highway robbers. Yet even in the midst of the imagery of God's new kingdom as a great city, we note that both a river and trees are central to that new city:

> Then the angel showed me the river of the water of life, as clear as crystal, flowing from the throne of God and of the Lamb down the middle of the great street of the city. On each side of the river stood the tree of life, bearing twelve crops of fruit, yielding its fruit every month. And the leaves of the tree are for the healing of the nations (Rev. 22:1–2).

The well-loved twenty-third psalm, attributed to David, begins with words of praise and acknowledgement: "The Lord is my shepherd, I lack nothing. He makes me lie down in green

pastures, he leads me beside quiet waters, he refreshes my soul."
In a fallen world full of stress, challenges, hardship, loss, and
sorrow, we all regularly need our souls restored. The psalmist
implicitly acknowledges that the world
wears us down. It's the reality of that
wearing down and of our resulting need
for restoration that makes the promise
of restoration so important. And how does
God restore our souls? David uses the
nature imagery of quiet water and
green pastures to describe the
soul-restoring and rest-inducing
work of the Lord, our Shepherd.
Now admittedly, drawing
only on this psalm to point toward
creation as the Creator's means
of soul restoration might be
making too much of this imagery.
For a shepherd-poet who had spent
years in charge of sheep, finding
green pastures would be an obvious
image of care. Likewise, for one living
in the arid landscapes of Israel, the image of quiet water would
also come naturally to portray restoration of the soul after a
harsh world has taken its toll. As a Vermonter living in the midst
of the Green Mountains, surrounded by lakes, rivers, ponds,
and streams, and by the vast and lush green pastures of the

Champlain Valley, the imagery that comes to my mind when I read Psalm 23 is quite different from what David had in mind. As a shepherd in those arid hills, David would have worked hard at times just to find a small bit of grass his sheep could munch on or a little spring trickling out of the rocks. When his poetic mind searched for imagery that conveyed his important ideas, these experiences would have come to mind. The green pastures and quiet waters he describes, then, could well have been primarily a metaphorical and not literal description of God's restoring work. I can think of a variety of times and places in my own life that God has used to grant me rest and peace: these have included a church sanctuary and the house of a friend as well as a flower garden, the woods behind my house, or a cabin in a state or national park. These are metaphorical green pastures and quiet waters, though not always literal ones.

At the same time, though, if we consider *only* a metaphorical understanding of Psalm 23, we might also be missing something important in God's restoring work—especially when seen in light of some of the passages listed above as well as the work of modern science on the health impacts of green spaces. Numerous studies over the past several years have provided strong evidence that time spent in green spaces—listening to birdsongs, observing animals, walking in the woods, and taking in aromas from plants—have tremendous health benefits related to our overall wellbeing: lowering our cortisol levels, reducing anxiety and mental fatigue, calming and relaxing us, and even reducing feelings of depression.

Experientially, I am not at all surprised by these studies. Long before I had seen the studies, I'd often benefited from times in green spaces; I could testify to the truth of the results. From a biblical perspective, I am even less surprised. God created our biological bodies, including our complex brains. He knows how they work. He knows the impact that these places—quiet waters and green growing things especially—have on us. God knew all along what modern science has only recently begun to conclude: nature restores our souls. So the literal quiet waters and green pastures of creation are often the best and most important places God leads us. The Creator who fashioned us out of the stuff of the earth also made water in all its forms. Genesis 1:2 speaks of God's spirit hovering over these quiet waters at the start of creation. He created a world with lakes, ponds, and lagoons. He also created the majestic spruce trees to surround them, the mountain peaks to guard them, and the green meadows that roll down to the shores.

Certainly, the view that nature is all peace and tranquility is profoundly naïve and can only be held by one who has spent little time in attentiveness to the natural world. As has often been noted, it is a dog-eat-dog world. It is also a fish-eat-fish, snake-eat-snake, and bird-eat-bird world, as well as a snake-eat-fish, bird-eat-snake, and even a fish-eat-bird world. This predatory violence in nature is one of the reasons why the prophecy of Isaiah 65:25 (and elsewhere) is so wonderful and startling:

> The wolf and the lamb will feed together,
>   and the lion will eat straw like the ox,
>   and dust will be the serpent's food.
> They will neither harm nor destroy
>   on all my holy mountain," says the Lord.

Yet God's created world is also full of immeasurable beauty everywhere we look—as well as everywhere we listen and smell: the tiny fairy bees pollinating a blossom no bigger than a grain of rice in my yard; the hermit thrush in the maple trees outside my window ushering in the dawn with their song; the mist clinging to the slopes of the Green Mountain National Forest on a frosty October morning; the huge gold and red eastern lubber grasshopper with its elaborately decorated armored joints, hopping along a railing in Big Cypress National Preserve, trying to get a closer look at the lens of my camera while I back away; and the five roseate spoonbills perched on a cypress branch, spreading their wings to catch the morning sun.

Certainly, if we look to nature alone and view *it* as our savior, we will be disappointed. But if we look to God as our shepherd and soul-restorer, we should not be surprised that he uses his creation—the beauty of his created world of trees, flowers, rivers, mountains, prairies, oceans, wetlands—to do his restoring work in us. Being attentive to creation is a way to know our Creator God more fully. It is a way to delight in him as we find wonder and join in creation's song of praise (Ps. 148). It is also a way to receive from God a great gift of rest and the restoration of our souls.

Agulukpak Morning

(Wood-Tikchik State Park, Alaska, July 2022)

In the morning, a moving ceiling
of clouds cuts off the peaks, creates
a gray-green, one-walled chamber
of Lake Beverly. Wind off the water
makes mosquitos disappear, hands
feel colder, coffee in the mug
seem hotter, heart more grateful.

Human anglers will soon appear,
but now a hunting osprey hovers,
mergansers dive, caddisflies dance
to a soundtrack of splashing sockeye,
the river rolling glacial gravel,
and the softer sough of a morning
breeze stirring branches on the shore.

A bald eagle, chased by crows, cruises
below the treetops, clenched talons
bearing breakfast back to the nest.
A dead salmon, nearly decayed, drifts down
the Agulukpak. A gull, afloat, pecks
at this feast too fine to pass up,
but too hefty to haul away.

I'm tempted to wade this quiet water,
casting flies of elk hair and hackle
to rising rainbow trout, but instead
I watch winged fishers hunt from high,
a bear sow with twins prowl the shore.
I leave the wild for a while undisturbed
as I listen, look, and breathe. Breathe.

Below, the river reflects cedar and birch
in charcoal-sketch smudges of blue
near patches of lacy parsnip
dotting a field of fireweed
in impressionistic brush strokes—
a carpet beneath the cloud ceiling
sheltering me in this room.

SOME QUIET WATERS

Having lived my whole life in the northern climate of New England and upstate New York, mostly in hilly or mountainous landscapes full of cold rivers and receiving plenty of winter weather, I'm not used to heat. Cold I can handle. Unless there is a brutal wind, I can generally be comfortable outdoors at least down to -10°F by wearing the proper attire: thick merino wool socks, long wool underwear beneath my pants, well-insulated boots and gloves (the kind made for warmth rather than style), and of course a heavy parka and a warm wool hat that goes snugly over my ears. Maybe a scarf, too, if it's windy. I've enjoyed outdoor activities including Nordic skiing in even colder weather. What I don't know how to handle is heat. When Deborah and I landed in Orlando, Florida, to visit Matt Clark and begin our in-person collaboration on this book, it was the tail end of a 98° day. As we made our way through the parking garage to get our rental car, Deborah and I both wondered why we had left Vermont on what (for us) had been a perfect May day: 72°, dry and sunny with a slight breeze, during our favorite time of the year when the leaves had just opened up to their early spring fresh yellow-green hues, trees and our favorite spring flowers were blossoming, and our yard was busy with a host of pollinators, including eastern tiger swallowtails and large, awkwardly beautiful (or beautifully awkward) bumblebees.

It had been a busy spring for me with a lot of speaking-related travel in addition to my full-time college teaching job.

Layered on top of that was a lot of uncertainty and anxiety—and many rounds of paperwork—surrounding an important and consequential Medicaid application for my father, who suffered from Alzheimer's disease. I was physically and emotionally tired and still trying to resist the temptation to anxiety. The oppressive Florida heat didn't help. Neither did the Orlando traffic.

The following morning after Matt left for his job teaching art and science at the Geneva School in Winter Park, Deborah and I hopped in the car and headed north toward the Ocala National Forest to spend the day. Driving through yet more city traffic, and not quite sure where we were going, I was still carrying some of my anxiety with me. Our first stop (after breakfast) was at Blue Spring State Park. We parked the rental car and walked down to where a short river winds from the park's eponymous spring a little under a half mile to the Saint Johns River. Stepping under the thick riparian shade of bald cypress and live oak trees—a canopy known in Florida wetlands as a *hammock*—I felt the tension melting away. Black anhingas with white-streaked wing feathers, spear-like beaks, and a light brown spiky hairdo, perched on tree branches above the river near long-necked cormorants. Wood ducks stood on logs just above the water. Several boat-tailed grackles flitted from tree to tree. One red-shouldered hawk soared in circles over the treetops, while another with large piercing eyes, an intimidating hooked raptor's beak, brown- and white-flecked wing feathers, and (yes) beautiful auburn shoulders came and landed just a few yards upstream of us on a thick branch draped with Spanish moss. We walked along the shaded boardwalk pausing frequently to look down into the water and just to be quiet and attentive. Turtles sunned on logs and rocks. A large number and variety of fish, including largemouth bass, long pointy gar, bowfin, catfish, and a few small tarpon, swam in the 72° crystal-clear water below us. A whitetail doe with her young

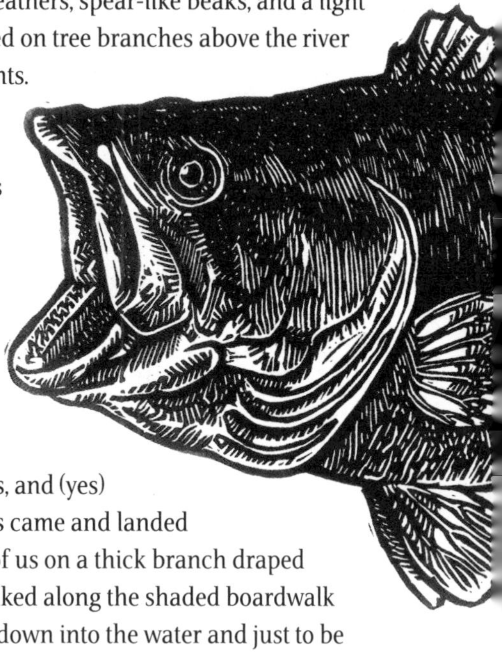

spotted fawn wandered along the depression to our right. High in the treetops, a trio of American black vultures kept their nostrils and eyes open for dead animals.

The scene filled me with wonder. One hundred million gallons of water pour out of Blue Spring every day. That volume is staggering. I had to read the number several times (and count the zeros) to be sure I wasn't misreading. That's as much water coming out of a single hole in the Florida ground as typically flows down either the New Haven River a couple miles north of my Vermont home or the Middlebury River a few miles to our south, both of which gather their waters from myriad springs and wetlands and rainfall over thousands of acres. Although we were too late in the year to see manatees, the knowledge that more than eight hundred of them had recently been in this same spot also filled me with wonder. The beauty of the majestic live oak trees and fascinating cypress trees, which stand on knobby knees with their roots under water, along with the variety of creatures many of which I had never seen before, filled me with delight as well. Hand in hand with the wonder and delight was a deep sense of peace and rest. It is not a stretch at all to say that standing beside that peaceful water and gazing into it was soul restoring. From both a biblical perspective and a perspective of modern science (including fields of psychology and neuroscience), I shouldn't be surprised by the restoration of the soul brought about by times spent in God's creation.

Three months after my visit to Florida, I sit with my Bible on the back deck of Eaglerock Cabin in Ernest Gruening State Historical Park with my daughter-in-law McKenna, on the first morning of a two-week collaborative artist residency with Alaska State Parks. The waters of Amalga Bay in front of me are surprisingly calm—calmer than many of the New England lakes and ponds where my wife and I paddle our canoes. Looking at the flat water, I have to remind myself that this is a reach of the Pacific Ocean.

Soon my eyes are drawn to three small shiny crows sitting on the rocks at the edge of the incoming tide in front of me. They appear to be looking for food in the intertidal zone. I wonder what they are hoping for. A crab in the seaweed, or perhaps a peck at one of the many salmon carcasses strewn along the rocks? Soon I see other crows moving back and forth across the bay. Two or three will head off to some spot or another, followed by several stragglers until six, seven, or eight have passed. Two minutes later, they fly back in the other direction like teenagers with FOMO (fear of missing out). Back and forth. Back and forth. Constantly chattering. They are expending lots of energy but don't seem to be accomplishing much. Yet sitting still and watching them, I find I am doing the opposite.

A little while later, too far away to see them in great detail or to identify the species, a flock of seven ducks makes their way across Amalga Bay. Unlike the crows, they keep in a tight cluster weaving in amongst each other. Above the waterline, their bodies are still and calm, but they are moving surprisingly fast. It takes only a few minutes for them to cross a large expanse of the bay. Meanwhile, the crows are still moving back and forth, trying not to miss out on whatever the others have found. Now there are eight of them on the rocks in front of me. Now there are none.

My eyes swing to my right, to the little cove where a small waterfall pours from a lagoon known as the Peterson Salt Chuck down into saltwater. Salmon are leaping all along the shoreline, especially around the mouth of the creek. I can see both chum and humpy salmon, distinguishable mostly by their coloring but also by their size and shape, with chum being the second largest of the five species of Pacific salmon that spawn in Alaska and pinks the smallest. In two adjacent pools in the short section of Peterson Creek above the tide, the chum salmon are thick as sardines in a can. I've been told that a black bear sow and two cubs have been visiting the section of creek for the easy hunting. Many salmon are dead on the rocks beside the stream. The females have had their eggs ripped out of them. They have all had their eyes pecked out by birds.

Because of the stench of their rot and their ugly mouths, ragged with teeth like a junkyard dog, I forget sometimes how beautiful chum salmon are when they first start to spawn.

While spawning Chinook, coho, and sockeye salmon all have sides that turn some shade of mostly solid red, and the humpies have horizontal stripes not unlike those of a rainbow trout, the chum salmon gain mottled vertical stripes of purple and green. Before they get far up into their spawn and start to rot, they are quite striking. But like all their Pacific salmon cousins, they have a driving instinct to reproduce, and they will die shortly after they succeed. Or in many cases—as when they become food for eagle or seal or hungry bear mama with cubs—they will die before that. The shore of the stream as well as the rocks along the edge of the bay are strewn with carcasses.

As morning clouds and mist rise, I finally catch a glimpse of
a line of snow-covered peaks on the far side of Lynn Canal, rising
four to nearly six thousand feet above sea level. These mountains
are part of the Chilkat Range and lie along the boundary
between Tongass National Forest and the eastern edge of Glacier
Bay National Park. The patterns of light and clouds along the
mountains are constantly changing. I will, over the next few days,
take hundreds of pictures of the same view, which is never really
the same view. At times clouds pour over the line of peaks and
down the near side, like whipped cream overflowing a bowl. My
awe-and-wonder meter registers at the very top of the scale. So
does my peace and rest meter.

Nearer at hand, my eyes are drawn to a different sort of
majesty: the giant Sitka spruce trees that line the shore, so
covered in moss and draped in witch's hair lichen that the tree
bark is barely visible except for on the south side below the
lowest branches. As I sit on the deck watching, a bald eagle lands
on the tree's highest branches. Though I watched it land and
know it is there, especially when it begins chittering at another
eagle across the little bay, I cannot see it through the mossy
lichen-draped branches. Yet I imagine it has a wonderful view
of the rocky shore at low tide, thirty feet down a steep bank. One
little patch of watermelon berries—dark-red ripe, like miniature
soft-skinned watermelons—grows near the base of the tree.
McKenna plucks a few berries and drops them into her yogurt-
and-granola breakfast. She makes a satisfied sound as their
sweet juice explodes in the mouth.

The following morning, I walk out of the cabin just as the skies are growing light and wander over to the outlet of the Peterson Salt Chuck where the chum salmon are spawning. I am hoping to see the sow black bear with her pair of spring cubs. Instead, a lone male black bear is foraging. He finds the hunting easy and apparently has soon had his fill. He disappears into the foliage on the near side of the creek. I wait and watch for several minutes, expecting him to reemerge where the salmon are and begin to hunt again. Then a movement behind me catches my attention, and I realize the bear has circled around through the woods (presumably to avoid me) and emerged thirty yards behind me. I watch as he continues down the shoreline.

Nature is not quiet. Even the waters that are to me so peaceful and soul-restoring are not always quiet. That is, figurately they are, but literally they are not. At low tide, the outlet of the salt check tumbles down fifteen or twenty feet through several pools and over cascades to reach the saltwater, making a constant low rumble. Only at high tide does the volume get quieter. Then, too, there is the racket from the large numbers of gulls and crows cawing and harping at one another as they peruse the rocks for some bit of not-yet-scavenged food. Now and then this ever-present crowd noise is interrupted by the more piercing cry of one of the several eagles that are always about, also looking for food. The eagles are more willing to hold still, perched on some tall rock or up in one of the spruce trees overlooking the little bay.

In the evening, though, after an unusually warm day, it does get quieter. Taking a break from my writing, I am standing near the outlet of the Salt Chuck casting flies for rising cutthroat trout when I see a black nose sticking out of the grass on the opposite bank. A bear inches out and looks at me for a long moment, then shyly withdraws. It wants some of that easy tasty treat waiting in the pool. Yet it is not aggressive. Since the bear is more dependent on the fish than I am, I leave the water and climb up on the bank several yards back to allow the bear to hunt without threat from me. A minute later the bear comes out and begins to fish in the pool. Unlike me, bears—including both black and brown—are not catch-and-release fishers. They are here for the food, not the sport. But while bears living near urban areas or campgrounds habituated by careless humans will often adjust to an unhealthy diet of easy-to-get junk food found in trashcans and careless campsites, healthy bears that have not adapted to human foods are much smarter. Because they live in the wild and have to survive a long Alaskan winter, they need to focus on the most nutritional-rich and protein-dense options they can get. They need this in order to be healthy. When it comes to salmon, especially when the salmon is plentiful, that means eating the eggs and sometimes the brains and organs. Bears will often catch a salmon, find that it is male, and discard it. They look instead for the egg-laden females.

I have on numerous occasions watched a brown bear rip a fish open with its claws, strip out and eat the eggs, and discard the flesh—the part of the salmon I would most want to eat, filleted and grilled. I surmise that this black bear is doing the same thing, for it quickly discards the first salmon it catches. A minute later it catches another. From across the river, I watch as it appears to open up the fish, eat something, and then leave the rest.

I have no doubt there is a spiritual lesson here in the contrast between these bears living as they should and the easy-to-get-junk-food-fed bears found in state parks in the east. There isn't anything wrong with salmon meat, but the bear knows it is worth working harder to get the eggs. I think how easy it is to eat spiritual junk food (or just junk food in general), or to spend our time and energy consuming entertainment that isn't necessarily inherently bad but isn't going to feed us. The healthy bears are willing to work hard to get food that will deeply nourish and sustain them.

The woods around the cabin are thick with berry bushes.
In addition to watermelon berries, I find red huckleberries,
blueberries, gooseberries, and thimbleberries. Most grow beneath
a thick canopy, in the midst of a temperate rainforest that doesn't
get a lot of sunlight. One blueberry bush might hold only a dozen
or two small ripe berries. It would take a lot of work to collect
enough for jam, but I stop now and then and pick handfuls to
bring home for my oatmeal or cereal the next morning.

A week after I arrive, my wife Deborah joins me for the
second half of my residency. My planned side trip to Glacier Bay
National Park was the bait that lured her out. We take a state
ferry from Juneau to Gustavus where a ten-mile bus ride brings
us into the park. After a night at the park lodge followed by an
early breakfast, we meet at the dock for an eight-hour tour of
Glacier Bay that will cover 120 miles of water all the way to the
tidewater Johns Hopkins Glacier and back. We see orcas and
humpback whales, hundreds of Stellar sea lions sunning on
rocks while barking, roaring, and jostling one another for prime
positions, one pod of porpoises, seals hauled out on an ice floe,
and a large brown bear grazing on bear berries along a steep
ledge. And all manner of sea birds, especially around South
Marble Island: Glaucous gulls with their gray wings, cormorants
diving and perched on ledges on steep white vertical cliffs, black
winged kittiwakes, murres, and the small, tufted puffins that
everybody wants to see, which are simultaneously adorably cute
and also ungainly when they use those made-for-diving wings to
fly through the air.

The mountains, which rise from sea level to more than fifteen thousand feet, are breathtaking. And so are the park's eponymous glaciers. Johns Hopkins Glacier is a mile wide at sea level and rises about three hundred feet above sea level. Every minute or two, we hear a thunderous crack like fireworks and watch a huge section of ice fall into the water as it calves. Flocks of gulls circle around the base of the glacier waiting for a sudden uprising of food stirred up from below each time the glacier calves. The exposed ledge on both sides of the glacier is its own work of art, painted with lichen and moss and little patches of dwarf fireweed, with rock twisted and gouged in shades of white, green, black, and gray by the tremendous weight of glaciers and the geological activity that thrust those mountain peaks so high. Though it was t-shirt weather back at the lodge, we bundle up in hats, gloves, and fleece as we stand on the deck in the icy wind blowing down off the glacier. Yet the cold mist doesn't dampen my spirits. If the needle of my awe-and-wonder meter had earlier been at the maximum reading, it has now broken past the right edge. Tears flow more freely than words.

And then there are the sea otters. According to the National Park Service website, the population of sea otters in Glacier Bay

has grown from zero to nine thousand in the last
twenty years. I believe it. They are everywhere.
We begin seeing them even before
our tour catamaran leaves the dock.
We see the densest numbers as we
make our way out of the small harbor.
Some are swimming quickly, leaving
wakes, perhaps making their way out to
feeding grounds for the day. Some are
floating on their backs, with their hind
toes sticking up in the air. They look very

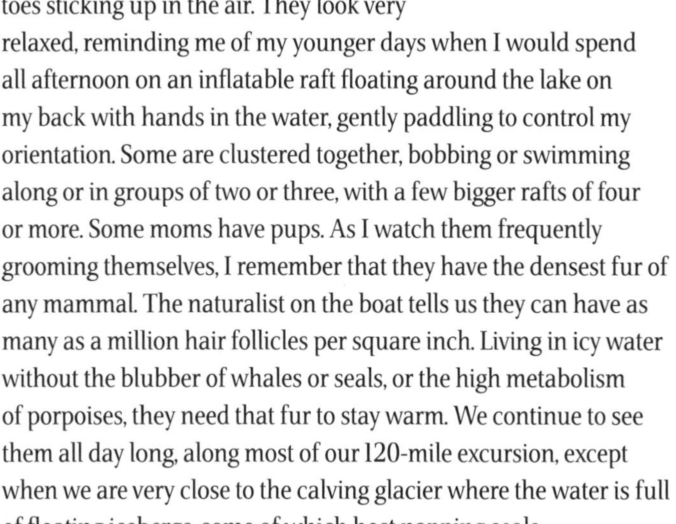

relaxed, reminding me of my younger days when I would spend
all afternoon on an inflatable raft floating around the lake on
my back with hands in the water, gently paddling to control my
orientation. Some are clustered together, bobbing or swimming
along or in groups of two or three, with a few bigger rafts of four
or more. Some moms have pups. As I watch them frequently
grooming themselves, I remember that they have the densest fur of
any mammal. The naturalist on the boat tells us they can have as
many as a million hair follicles per square inch. Living in icy water
without the blubber of whales or seals, or the high metabolism
of porpoises, they need that fur to stay warm. We continue to see
them all day long, along most of our 120-mile excursion, except
when we are very close to the calving glacier where the water is full
of floating icebergs, some of which host napping seals.

Back at Eaglerock Cabin on my last full day of our residency,
I wake at 4:30 a.m. to bring Deborah to the airport for her flight

home. When I return around 6:30 a.m., I walk down again to the outlet of the lagoon. To my delight, I see the sow bear hunting in the first little pool above the waterfall, which after nearly two weeks of hot dry weather has gotten very shallow with just a small stream of water trickling through. I watch her from behind the trees for a minute or two before I notice her cubs in the shadows on the far side of the pool. Although there have been signs and sightings from daily visits, the only previous time I saw her with her cubs, she had gotten startled and run off into the woods. This time, however, she doesn't seem to mind my presence at a safe distance away in the trees atop the bank, despite two other human voices speaking down on the rocks below the pool. After a couple minutes of fishing, she wanders over to fetch her cubs. They follow her into the pool and attempt some hunting on their own. There are not many salmon left, however—only a few old half-rotted chum. No fresh pinks have yet pushed in from the saltwater. It will take a higher tide than we've had in the past few days to lift them over the falls.

The sow starts looking in my direction as though she wants to come up the trail instead of disappearing into the woods as she did when I saw her before. Sensitive to the demands of single parenting, and the short season she has for storing up a lot of fat reserves for when food is less plentiful, I begin to back away up the trail so she has a clear path to walk wherever she wants. She calls her cubs with a series of soft hoots, and when I have gone another thirty yards up the trail, she comes up the hill and starts moving slowly in my direction. She is not threatening or at all aggressive, but rather cautious with her cubs. I continue to back up and she makes her way up the trail, with her cubs following behind. Eventually, she turns off the trail with her cubs and disappears into the brush back toward the water.

Although the woods around my house may be the place where I regularly find the needed times of quiet and rest, I have been fortunate to have had my soul restored in some places of overwhelming beauty. It is a mystery that the same places whose spectacular and majestic beauty bring such wonder and awe can also bring such soul-restoring rest. I will leave that mystery unsolved for a time and simply accept it as grace.

Limnephilidea

"Chocolate and cream" caddisflies
rise off the slow-moving river
so thick and fast it feels
like a blizzard moving backward
through time.

Attentiveness and Christian Vocation: The Holy Work of Creation Care

The Lord said to Moses, "Tell Aaron and his sons,
'This is how you are to bless the Israelites. Say to them:
"The Lord bless you and keep you; the Lord make his face
shine on you and be gracious to you; the Lord turn
his face toward you and give you peace."'"
—Numbers 6:22–26

And the Lord God took the man, and put him
into the garden of Eden to dress it and to keep it.
—Genesis 2:15 (KJV)

I wasn't involved in a lot of after-school activities in the rural high school I attended as a teenager. In the winter, I raced on the alpine and cross-country ski teams (though I was at best a mediocre skier), and one spring I had a very minor role in the school musical, but that was the sum of all my extracurriculars. Most days I rode the first bus home as soon as school ended, grabbed a snack, and headed out into the hundreds of acres of woods, meadows, and wetlands surrounding our house: I would go over the hill behind our house to a secluded pond to fish for bass and panfish, or I would head down our quiet dead-end road to a small marshy wetland to look for frogs and turtles. I suppose some of my love of creation and my practices of attentiveness go back to those long school-day afternoons in middle school and high school, though I certainly hadn't formed any theology of creation at the time.

I did sing in the high school chorus for four years. Although it counted as a class that met during the regular school day, we had to perform occasional concerts outside of school hours, including the graduation ceremony at which we sang the same song every year: a blessing on the graduating seniors. Though it's been more than four decades since I was in high school and I've long ago forgotten most of the music we sang, the words and melody of that one song still echo in my head: "The Lord bless you and keep you. The Lord lift his countenance upon you. And give you peace. (And give you peace. And give you peace. And give you peace. The Lord make his face to shine upon you.)" Though the blessing sounded biblical, it was not until years later that I learned that the text was adapted by Peter Lutkin (1858-1931) from the English translation of Numbers 6:24–26, which are the words God gave to Moses's brother Aaron and his sons, the priests of Israel, to use as a blessing for the people of Israel. These verses are thus referred to as the Aaronic blessing. The Hebrew word translated to "keep" in this blessing is *shamar*. I am told by Hebrew scholars that *shamar* implies a loving, caring, sustaining kind of keeping: precisely the sort of keeping and blessing the Israelites would desire from God—and indeed a blessing which we might also desire today.

Genesis 2:15 also uses the word *shamar* to describe Adam's God-given vocation. The New International translation of this verse reads, "The Lord God took the man and put him in the Garden of Eden to work it and *take care of* [*shamar*] it." The King James translation of this verse makes clearer the connection to the *shamar* of the Aaronic blessing in Numbers 6:24–26 that we sang in our high school chorus: "And the Lord God took the man, and put him into the garden of Eden to dress it and to *keep* [*shamar*] it." The implications of the use of the word *shamar* in Genesis are profound. God's purpose for Adam was that he "take care of" creation with the same sort of loving, caring, sustaining kind of keeping that would be a blessing for the Israelites themselves. That is to say, Adam was not to exploit creation, and certainly not to destroy it, but rather to help it flourish and be fruitful. It is also important to note that the word *adam* is the Hebrew word for man. It may be related to the Hebrew word *adamah* which means "ground." It can be understood as either a proper noun ("Adam") or translated as a common noun ("the man").

So this mandate to care for creation in a way that blesses it and helps it flourish should really understood as a vocational statement for *all* humankind, for the man Adam was our archetype.

This is certainly consistent with the previous chapter of Genesis. In Genesis 1 we read how God repeatedly proclaimed the rest of creation "good" even before placing humans on the scene. And though Genesis 1:28 states that our stewardship over creation implies authority, the immediately preceding verse (Genesis 1:27) provides a context for that authority: we are God's image-bearers. Thus our human authority is to be exercised in the image of God. This suggests that our authority as caretakers of creation ought to be exercised both in imitation of God's character, and also with God's purposes. And as the

creation account already made clear before this responsibility of authority was given, God's purposes include the fruitfulness and flourishing of all creation. We can see this especially in Genesis 1:22 when living creatures appear in creation: "God blessed them and said, 'Be fruitful and increase in number and fill the water in the seas, and let the birds increase on the earth.'" God desires living creatures to be blessed and to be fruitful. This is God's purpose for creation, and this purpose existed and was stated *before* humankind appeared on the scene, just as the goodness of creation was also repeatedly proclaimed *before* the arrival of humans.

Likewise, we have also seen indications of God's purposes in Psalm 104, which speaks of God's bringing about the flourishing of wild creatures and landscapes that seem to have no economic or agricultural value to us humans and not merely in ways useful to humankind. This psalm also paints a picture of God's attentiveness to his creatures, knowing the needs of each. Psalm 65:9–13 expresses something similar about God's care for creation, beyond simply its usefulness to humans:

> You care for the land and water it;
> you enrich it abundantly.
> The streams of God are filled with water
> to provide the people with grain,
> for so you have ordained it.
> You drench its furrows and level its ridges;
> you soften it with showers and bless its crops.
> You crown the year with your bounty,
> and your carts overflow with abundance.
> The grasslands of the wilderness overflow;
> the hills are clothed with gladness.
> The meadows are covered with flocks
> and the valleys are mantled with grain;
> they shout for joy and sing.

God also speaks prophetically through the psalmist in Psalm 50:11, saying, "I know every bird in the mountains, and the insects in the fields are mine." Not only does this remind us that all of creation still belongs to God and that we have authority as stewards only; it also reminds us of God's intimate knowing of creation—a knowing that helps us understand why we see such a clear picture of God attentiveness to and care for creation in Psalms 65 and 104.

We even see God's care for the flourishing of creation in the mandate for a Sabbath rest for all creation. God's command of a Sabbath day (Ex. 20:10; Deut. 5:14) was intended to apply to animals as well as humans. God even commanded that the land itself—that is, the soil—be given a Sabbath *year* of rest from tilling and planting every seventh year (Ex. 23:10–11; Lev. 25:1–7; Neh. 10:31). Jesus' own teaching speaks of the Father's care even for the lowly sparrow. Echoing an idea he shared in the Sermon on the Mount, Jesus later added: "Are not two sparrows sold for a penny? Yet not one of them will fall to the ground outside your Father's care" (Matt. 10:29). The rest of the Scriptures also continue to reveal just what God's example of authority is like, most especially through the person of Jesus who repeatedly

demonstrated and taught that we lead (or exercise authority) by being loving servants. Philippians 2 is a wonderful description of what that looks like. An implication is that our practice of authority over creation should be in that same image—the way Jesus demonstrated his own authority.

Not long ago I was thinking again about the care-taking task of humankind in the garden of Eden. One initial aspect of that task was naming all the living creatures: birds and wild animals as well as livestock (Gen. 2:19–20). Halfway through my high school career, Bob Dylan released his famous album *Slow Train Coming*. Although it would take me many years to fully appreciate the album, it still had an imaginative influence on my thinking as I slowly matured into adulthood. Until recently, I interpreted the naming of animals in Genesis 2 in light of Dylan's song from that album, "Man Gave Name To All The Animals," in which Adam's naming of animals is understood as referring to their common species name. *This one's a cow. I'll name that one a pig. And the one over there I'll call a sheep.* But think for a moment about some of the important biblical stories in which God names (or renames) people. God renamed Abram to Abraham, Sarai to Sarah, and Jacob to Israel. He gave to Simon the new name Peter.

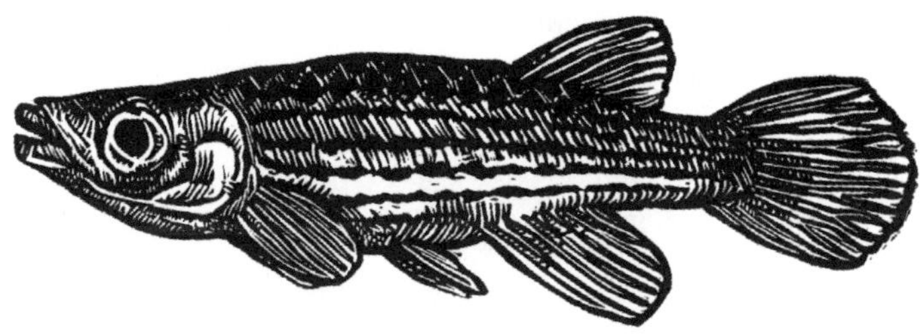

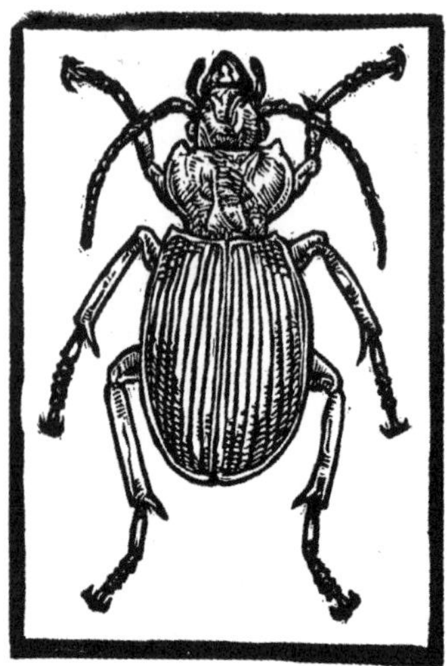 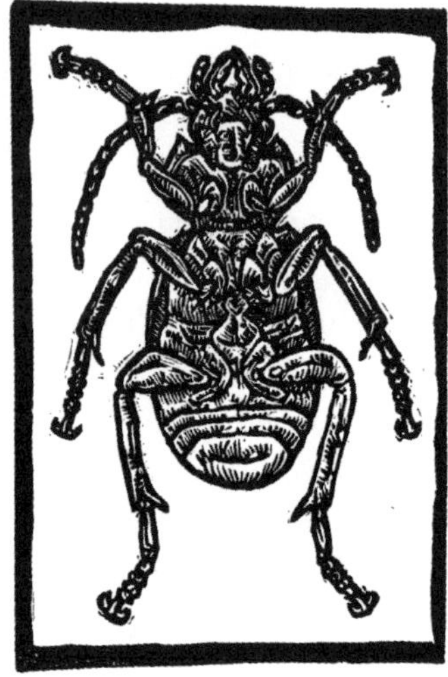

He told Zechariah to name his son John. (I suspect the title "the Baptist" was not part of his name when he emerged from the womb.) These are all proper names. That is, they are individual names, not species names. And each of these names contains a particular meaning. There is a wonderful intimacy involved in the sort of naming that comes out of God's intimate knowledge of the person, or the calling of that person, who is being named. I wonder if it is this sort of naming that Adam was called to do for the animals: to be attentive not just to the species but even to the individual creatures and out of that attentiveness to choose appropriate names. *That bull there is really strong—let's name him Daniel. And listen to how that crow is always laughing and cackling at us. I love his infectious humor. I will name him Isaac. And the*

big old tortoise comes by every day and just sits on the ground unmoving, waiting for me to give him a bite of fruit. It is such a solid rock! I've got to name him Peter.

Again, this relates directly to attentiveness. One important reason to pay attention to God's creation—what we often refer to as "nature"—is so that we better know how to care for it as we live out the fundamental calling God has given to his image-bearing human creatures whom he put on earth to be his stewards in charge of creation care. This is not a new concept. Good and loving parents know that to care for their own children they must know and love those children; they must be attentive to them to understand their needs as well as their personalities. And parenthood is a good metaphor in other ways, too, since caring for children also involves responsibility for them which in turn implies a certain authority over them: one that should be exercised as loving servants rather than as harsh dictators. Likewise, the care of a pastor for their church flock requires attentiveness if that flock is to truly flourish. When we voluntarily submit to our spouses—as both husbands and wives are called to do for each other (Eph. 5:21)—we have

in a sense given our spouses authority which we hope is exercised with attentiveness to us and a goal of our own flourishing.

If we are to be God's image-bearers in our authority over and care for creation, we should imitate God by showing a similar sort of attentiveness and care for flourishing, though of course in our case we must do so within the limits of our own finitude. And unlike the case in Genesis 2, when the authority and responsibility were first given to humankind, we now must exercise that attentive care in the midst of a fallen world—a topic we will return to in the final chapter.

Catching Crayfish

A crayfish stands on the dock, claws extended, seemingly undaunted by the giants who glare down at it. My two-year-old grandson is enthralled, simultaneously cowed by those threatening claws and also drawn to them in wonder and delight, wanting to reach down and touch the fascinating creature. And so it begins again, with a third generation of Dickerson youth sitting on a dock on this same lakefront, catching crayfish along the shoreline, watching them walk about on dry land for a few brief moments, or for perhaps a little longer in a bucket of water, and then sending them scurrying back to their homes.

I am constantly amazed by the bold little creatures. Though they typically weigh less than an ounce and measure perhaps three to four inches long, they nonetheless stand their ground against human creatures who are ten to twenty-five times as tall as they are long and several thousand times heavier. (Tasmanian crayfish may grow up to two feet long and weight ten pounds. Thankfully, we have none of these at the Maine lake where our family goes, or I might give up swimming there!) Perhaps the scale difference is so great that these little crustaceans don't even register how large even my two-year-old grandson is in comparison. I don't know how they see out of their compound eyes with thousands of eyelets—more like an insect eye than that of a typical vertebrate—or what their brains are able to comprehend. Maybe they see only my hand and not my whole body. It's still quite a display of bravery, since just my hand alone would be to them like a great giant. And despite the knowledge that I can barely feel the pinch of a four-inch crayfish, those brave little claws still cause my hand to jump back. I understand my grandson's hesitancy to reach out and touch one. And nearly sixty years after my own first crayfish encounters on this lake, I continue to experience with my grandsons a sense of wonder and delight at the common little crayfish. When I look at a crayfish, I can't help but think that God has a sense of humor.

I used to think of crayfish as a single ubiquitous species, like crows or bald eagles, that could found from the wetlands of the Gulf Coast (where folks call them crawdads) all the way up to cold New England lakes and streams, where they spend months under the ice. But worldwide there are more than five hundred species of crayfish with over 350 species in the United States alone. They come in colors of blue, red, brown, gray, yellow, and even bone white, with species that live in underground caves and never see daylight. Crayfish flourish in clean waters of all kinds, from lakes and rivers to small streams to swamps. They die in polluted waters.

These omnivorous scavengers can eat almost anything they can put into their mouths, though they (not unlike us humans) thrive when their diets are varied. One of my brothers recalls catching a crayfish and putting it into a fish tank with his goldfish. For days, the crayfish would wave its claws futilely at the passing goldfish, much larger than itself, as though trying to catch it. Or perhaps not so futilely: one day the little fellow managed to catch a hold of the passing fish with its claws. The scared fish took off at full speed with the crayfish holding on for all it was worth. Eventually the fish tired from dragging around the extra weight, and the crayfish, still clinging to a fish fin with one claw, began to reach into the fish's gills with its free claw and to dine. Crayfish can also eat mud and filter out the food in the detritus.

Even as crayfish can eat almost anything, including plant matter as well as animal matter, so too do many other creatures enjoy eating crayfish. Restaurants, especially in the southern United States, serve them to humans as gourmet delicacies. Many species of fish enjoy dining on them also. As a young teenager fishing old quarries of southern Indiana with my Great Uncle Bill, we'd catch buckets of crayfish and use them as bait for crappies and bass. Otters, racoons, and various wading birds also consume them. So do other crayfish. One of the biggest threats to native crayfish are human-introduced, non-native crayfish species.

Taxonomically, they are classified in the phylum *Arthropoda* (which includes invertebrates with an exoskeleton and jointed feet such as insects and crustaceans). They belong to the order *Decapoda*, which means "ten feet." The front pair of feet are the

weapons and hunting tools: that is, the pair with the large claws. The front two pairs of walking legs are also armed with small pinchers, used for eating and grooming as well as walking. The five hundred different crayfish species come from a variety of genera and even multiple taxonomic families. They breathe through gills and thus need to live in the water, but they can survive for periods out of water. On more than one occasion, we have found crayfish on our lawn dozens of feet from the pond, presumably in search of new waterbodies to colonize.

At least once a summer (and most years more often than that—first as a child, then as a teenager, then as a parent, and more recently as a grandparent), I have spent the better part of a hot summer morning catching crayfish and watching them move around and interact with one another in a large bucket. Catching them is as fun as watching them. From time to time, especially in the morning or late evening, we might spot them out walking the lake bottom in shallow water looking for food. The remains of a trout dinner is always a good way to attract a whole host of crayfish. But the most fun way to catch them is to tilt up rocks, especially the kind sitting on top of other rocks with gaps underneath, and attempt to grab the crayfish with bare hands. Most such rocks hide a crayfish or two, and most of those crayfish are able to escape within moments of being spotted by propelling themselves backwards with their strong tails. Sometimes they escape because I'm just too slow compared to their impressive tails, but often they are aided by my ingrained fear of those tiny but intimidating claws, which causes my hand to pull back involuntarily just before I grab them. "Back off," they seem to be saying with those upraised claws. I hesitate just a moment, and then *zip:* with a motion of their tails they jet off backward.

Since crayfish spend a lot of time in the darkness beneath rocks or in the murky, mucky darkness of swamp or lake bottom, and because many species are nocturnal, they have two pairs of antennae in addition to their compound eyes. One pair is used for feeling around in the dark, not unlike a cat's whiskers. The other smaller pair have chemical sensors to "taste" or "smell" for food. So I was delighted to learn, while writing this chapter, that the name "crayfish" is believed to come from an Old French word for "crevice"—a description of the favorite hideout of these little clawed creatures. The name is likely related to the word for crabs, another decapod known for its preference for caves and crevices, though crayfish are actually more closely related to American lobsters—the largest crustaceans in the world, whose claws truly are intimidating,

The study of crayfish is called *astacology*.

It's a study, I assume, that emerges from wonder and delight: a study in its deepest form that should lead to worship of the Creator of crustaceans.

Scene at the Orlando Wetland, May 2024

A great blue heron wades across the marsh

knee deep (on knees that bend reverse of mine)

alert to food or threat. Its world is harsh.

Now it waits in stillness for a chance to dine

on careless passersby: on frogs or fish

or alligator hatchlings, nine-inches long,

that wiggle down the throat, a favorite dish.

There's danger in the hunt. Things can go wrong.

A gator mama out to feed its throng

may lie in wait, young hatchlings as the bait.

I wonder that the heron does not mind
the six-foot gator coming from behind
with eager eyes. Perhaps the giant beast
believes the bird too swift to catch a-snooze—
a waste of breath to try and lunge, though prey
seems unaware—and goes on with its cruise.
Or does the reptile still recall the day
when gator was the menu at the feast?
And though it now be larger forty-fold,
do childhood fears still maintain their hold?

Spotted Joe Pye Weed and Eastern Swallowtails

It's blackberry season. Thanks to some disturbed habitats in the forest around our home, our woods are currently full of wild blackberries. Although I don't know for sure what cultivar these wild blackberries originally spread from, according to the Native Plant Trust there is at least one variety of blackberry believed to be native to the region—*Rubus vermontanus.* In fact, it gets its Latin name from our state. Whatever the variety, they have overtaken the wild raspberries that were abundant two years ago. Based on how quickly and widely the blackberry bushes have spread in the past four years, I am positive that the local bird population has been feasting on them, although I hear rather than see birds—especially veeries and red-eyed vireos—on our walks past that part of the woods. There are also signs that the neighborhood black bear regularly enjoys them.

This summer, with a steady mix of rain and sun, the blackberry bushes are thriving and the wild crop is quite good. The plants are flourishing so much, in fact, that in places we have to be careful on our trails or those long leaning vines will grab our clothing—or our arms, legs, and hair—as we walk by. I have gained a few scratches over the past few days carrying containers with me on my walks so that I can bring back a few handfuls of fresh wild berries. Because they are smaller than cultivated blackberries, and less dense on the bush since they are growing in the shade of the forest, it takes more effort to pick large amounts. Nonetheless, they have graced our breakfast cereal a few times and added flavor to yesterday's pancakes. By last night our supply had grown enough for me to make a large batch of blackberry-blueberry cobbler, which we shared with friends served right out of the oven topped with strawberry ice cream.

Birds looking for berries in the local woods will also find berries of the common buckthorn tree (*Rhamnus cathartica*). Unfortunately, those berries have a laxative effect. (Thankfully, I learned about this through reading and not through personal experience—although those who studied Latin might have guessed this from the species name *cathartica* which can mean "purgative.") The common buckthorn tree is not native to North America. It was introduced in the 1800s. But the laxative effect of its berries, which is unhealthy for the birds that eat them, turns out to be a very effective way for the tree to reproduce, since it results in the birds eating and spreading large numbers of seeds. As a result, the tree has spread invasively over large parts of the northeastern and north central United States where it can form a dense understory that, by shading out native plants and reducing wildlife habitat, offers little benefit and much harm. Varieties of Asian bush honeysuckle, another

non-native plant that has spread widely across my home state
of Vermont, is almost as bad. Though its berries don't have the
same laxative effect, they are poor in fats and not as nutritious
for birds as the native honeysuckle plants they have displaced.
Furthermore, they crowd out native plants that provide better
cover for nesting birds, leaving birds more susceptible to
predation. If you take a walk in almost any direction from my

house, you are likely to find
both of these plants within a
few hundred yards (though
you won't find as many as you
would have a few years ago).

Earlier I wrote about
my regular walks along
the trails around our
home with Deborah and
our dog Coda, and about
Deborah's wonderful

model of attentiveness: how I have better come to know
the plants and especially the spring ephemerals that grace
our woods. In addition to our native plants, Deborah is also
attentive to where the worst of the harmful invasive plants are
spreading—especially buckthorn, Japanese barberry, Asian bush
honeysuckle, garlic mustard, and oriental bittersweet. Although
the task of removing the larger buckthorn trees falls to me and
my larger chainsaw, Deborah has been on a crusade to remove
the other invasives and has acquired some tools for doing so:

an Extractigator, a Parsnip Predator, and most recently her own small electric chainsaw. We still have a long way to go. There are places where the invasive honeysuckle has completely taken over. Nonetheless, because of Deborah's attentive care, the forests around our home and the creatures who live there are healthier. Along many stretches of our walking trail not a barberry or invasive honeysuckle can be found. Native plants are now filling that space.

When we moved to our home twenty-five years ago, there were several majestic butternuts within a few hundred yards of our house that produced large crops each year, but they died of blight within our first decade there. The next to go were our beautiful

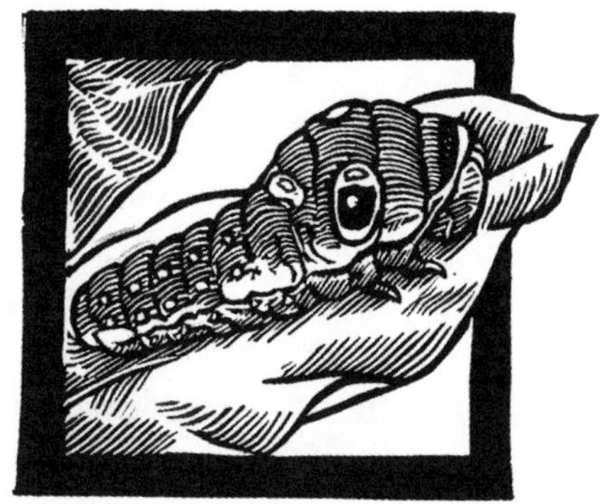

beeches—producers of a favorite food for the local bear, deer, and wild turkeys. In the past fifteen years, we have lost most of our beeches to blight. One of the things I take note of as I walk is the condition of those that remain in one small section of our forest where several still seem to be thriving. Now that the emerald ash borer beetle has reached our area, we are losing our ash trees also. Our hemlocks might not be around for many more years as the hemlock woody adelgid has reached Vermont and is slowly making its way north, killing all the hemlocks on its march.

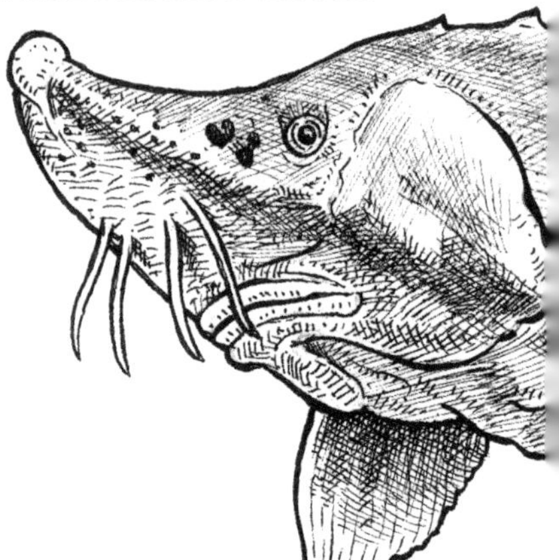

Our house is a little over fifty years old. I think it was built as a seasonal home or hunting camp, since the pipes were designed to be drained before winter. It has no foundation or basement; it was built on top of a dozen concrete pylons set on ledge. One wing of the house with a bedroom and attached dirt-floor garage was built directly on rocks. Not surprisingly, a few years ago we had to tear down that wing as it decayed. We replaced it with a new detached garage and in-law apartment—a building which we now live in, though we are not in-laws of anybody living in the other part of the house, which we rent out. As the excavators dug down to ledge to put in an actual basement on the new building, we had to take down a couple of old pine trees and displace a lot of soil. At the end of the construction, we had a backyard of bare dirt. The builders seeded it with grass, but a few days later, before the grass could take root, a thunderstorm washed all the seed away. Rather than reseed with non-native grass, which to most wild creatures including native insects and other pollinators is a food desert (not to be confused with a dessert), I decided to plant the yard with a mix of clovers and wildflowers and to leave the lawn unmowed for wildlife. I later read about native plants that are particularly friendly to native pollinators, especially moths and butterflies, which are also an important food sources to many wild birds. I added some additional native plants including dwarf wild columbine (*Aquilegia canadensis*—also called "little lanterns"), spotted joe pye weed (*Eutrochium maculatum*), swamp milkweed (*Asclepias incarnata*), and Bowman's root (*Gillenia trifoliata*). Initially, I only planned to leave the lawn unmowed through May, thus joining the "No Mow May" movement. But when June rolled around that first year after planting, I began to see a wonderful abundance of pollinators in the yard, including numerous varieties of butterflies such eastern tiger swallowtails, giant swallowtails, and even occasionally some monarchs, as well as bumblebees and other native bees. That swallowtails are common does not make them any less beautiful or wondrous. What from a distance may just appear a blur of yellow and black, from up close proves to be an intricate pattern of stripes, lines, curves, and filigree, with highlights of blue along the tail and even little orange accessories like tiny earrings. Whenever one flutters by, I pause what I'm doing and gaze in wonder and admiration. Who other than God could have painted such art?

Although I think my decision to leave my yard unmowed throughout the summer was motivated by a desire to practice *shamar* for creation, including

caring for the birds and the butterflies, I have to acknowledge that the increased opportunity to delight in the beauty of lepidoptera didn't hurt.

As the population of butterflies, moths, and bees grew, I also began to notice a variety of birds I had never before seen around our yard. A gray catbird began hanging out (and singing) on an old dead pine overlooking the yard, between hunting forays down in the grasses. One ground-nesting bird in the LBB (Little Brown Bird) category even built a nest and laid its eggs right in the middle of the yard, in a particularly thick and tall patch of grasses. Despite many efforts to get close enough to identify it or to get a picture, I was never completely sure which LBB it was, though Savannah sparrow was my best guess. I also started hearing calls of both wood thrush and hermit thrush (Vermont's state bird) right on the edge of the yard, instead of far away in the forest. Varieties of warblers (black-throated, black-and-white, and green-sided) and vireos (both red-eyed and blue-headed) also became common around the yard, along with veeries—although (like the varieties of thrush) I heard rather than saw them, especially in the summer mornings at sunrise when our bedroom window is often open. This year, a scarlet tanager which feeds primarily on pollinators showed up and spent the summer by our house. Deborah noted one bird that became a regular visitor to our back door, and realized it was grabbing slugs off the wet ground below our eaves. I have no doubt that the planting of native plants, which led to the increase in native pollinators, was a significant reason for the increase in numbers and varieties of our backyard birds.

Next year I plan to research and plant more native plants, and also to be intentional about recording moth, butterfly, and bird sightings so I can be more aware of which native insects these plants are attracting and which birds are following those insects in.

Scene on the Cobboseecontee

"Hundreds of Atlantic sturgeon have turned up in a stream in downtown Gardiner, giving local residents a rare, close-up glimpse of the massive fish . . . Folks who have lived in town for the whole lives have never seen anything like it."—Maine Public.

Observers on a bridge in Gardiner Maine
gazed down into a rushing river, grinning
at the mighty fish below them finning
in a current swelled from days of rain.
Atlantic sturgeon eight feet long (or more)
returned to where they long ago had spawned:
a flow from which they had for longbeen gone.
but could this day again be seen from shore
and bridge: whose Wabenaki name means "place
of many sturgeon." What some dared to dream –
restoring of a once-fragmented stream –
had come to pass. Displaced and then erased,
swimming dinosaurs returned to town
where stewards took the Edwards Dam right down.

All Creation Groans:
Lamenting with Creation
as a Holy Vocation

We know that the whole creation has been groaning
as in the pains of childbirth right up to the present time.
—Romans 8:22

The Lord Almighty is speaking through his prophet Jeremiah, describing the punishment that will come to Israel. This punishment, God says through the prophet, is "because of the sin of my people" (Jer. 9:7). Then, in the midst of describing the many sins for which Israelites have earned punishment, God's voice suddenly turns to lament.

I will weep and wail for the mountains
and take up a lament concerning
the wilderness grasslands.
They are desolate and untraveled,
and the lowing of cattle is not heard.
The birds have all fled
and the animals are gone. (Jeremiah 9:10)

It is a beautiful and moving passage as God mourns over the destruction and suffering of creation—a passage that reveals God's love for the whole world, including all the creatures he has made. For readers conditioned to think that God cares *only* for humans, or that any value in nature is found only its usefulness to humankind, it is important to note that God's lament—in a way reminiscent of Psalm 104—begins with the weeping and wailing for the desolation of the mountains and wilderness, which to the Israelites of the day were places of little or no economic or agricultural use. God then also laments not only the disappearance of cattle (creatures of value to Israelite herders) but also the disappearance of birds and other animals—those that are presumably not in the category of the "cattle" just mentioned.

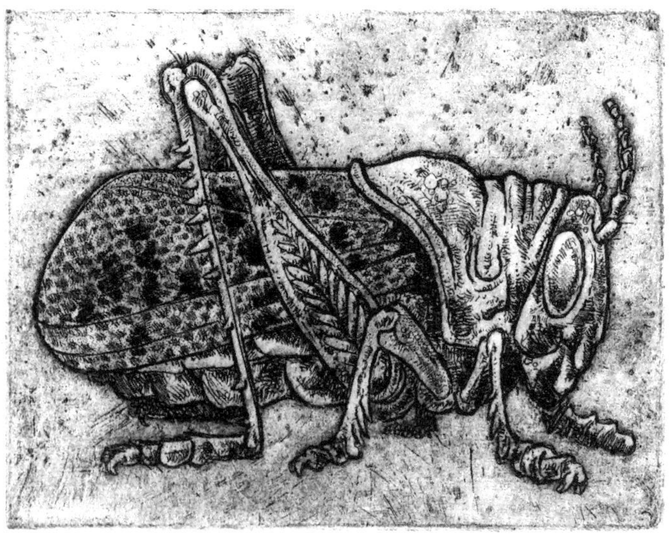

Jeremiah seems to understand God's lament at the desolation of the non-human world caused by human sin and wickedness and turns it into his own lament, asking "How long will the land lie parched and the grass in every field be withered? Because those who live in it are wicked, the animals and birds have perished." He goes on to complain even further that the humans whose wickedness has caused such destruction to creation wrongly think that God doesn't care and therefore they will get away with it. "Moreover, the people are saying, 'He will not see what happens to us'" (Jer. 12:4). We see something similar in God's word spoken through the prophet Joel. In Joel 1, after God foretells as punishment for the sin of Israel a plague of locusts devouring Israel's vineyards and grainfields, God then calls Israel to lament. Since the words in verse 19 are addressed to God, I read the lament in Joel 1:16–20 as Joel's response. As with Jeremiah, Joel speaks not only of the dried-up grain and of the suffering of sheep and cattle (17–18), but he goes on to lament for the suffering of trees and wild animals:

> To you, Lord, I call,
>> for fire has devoured the pastures in the wilderness
>> and flames have burned up all the trees of the field.
> Even the wild animals pant for you;
>> the streams of water have dried up
>> and fire has devoured the pastures in the wilderness.
> (19–20)

Reading these laments, all while I look around at how nature continues to suffer today, I often find myself in lament as well, grieving at the destruction of God's creative work that results from human sin and rebellion.

I grew up near three rivers. Although I never spent time *in* any of their waters, nor even paid much attention to them, all three shaped my environment and therefore shaped my growing up. I started life in the city of Cambridge, Massachusetts, which is bounded on the south by the Charles River. My father worked for a Christian ministry on some university campuses right by the river. After we moved out of Cambridge to a rural town west of the city, he started a small independent bookstore in Harvard Square just a couple blocks from the river. When I was in elementary and middle school, I regularly went to work with him. Depending on which route we took on a given morning, the last portion of the commute was either along Memorial Drive or Soldier's Field Road, both of which ran along the Charles. Some days I would walk over to the river during breaks. Historically, the Charles was plagued by sewage discharge, toxic industrial chemicals, and urban runoff. According to the EPA, as late as 2006 there were still billions of gallons a year of combined sewage overflows dumped into it. I remember hearing as a young adult that if somebody fell in—for example during one of the city's famous crew races—the contamination would be so bad the person would be rushed to the hospital. Although my father started taking me on regular fishing trips when I was in third grade, the Charles was not a place we would ever have fished despite proximity to it.

During the transition period moving away from Cambridge, we lived briefly in a tiny village in western Maine: an old mill town in the foothills of the White Mountains. I went to kindergarten just a few miles from the Androscoggin River, the second of those three rivers in my life. In 1972, *Time* magazine listed the Androscoggin as one of the ten filthiest rivers in the entire United States. Where it flowed through the neighboring town, it was full of both raw sewage and toxic effluent from several pulp mills upriver. Downstream of our house, the Androscoggin got even

worse as it picked up agricultural pesticides and fertilizers from numerous farms along the river valley, along with more paper mill refuse in the city of Rumford. Although we would continue to spend time in that area through the rest of my growing up years, I never fished that river either, nor even put a finger in it. And things got no better when our house in central Massachusetts was completed and we moved in halfway through my kindergarten year. The Nashua River, which ran along the edge of that town, once appeared in *National Geographic* as the icon of the country's polluted rivers. Although by the time I was a teenager my fishing explorations began to take me to numerous lakes, ponds, rivers, and streams in the area, the Nashua wasn't one of them.

It is perhaps not surprising that in my childhood I was largely unfamiliar with wading birds and waterfowl except for the ducks that swam in ponds on the Boston Commons, living on unhealthy handouts of bread and crackers. I never saw a bald eagle or watched an osprey dive. No green herons or little blue herons or even any great blue herons visited those three rivers. I never heard the song of a loon or the guttural call of an American bittern.

Just before my ninth birthday, however, my father took me on a five-day camping trip on the newly designated Allagash Wilderness Waterway in northern Maine. There, in the clean lakes and rivers of that protected watershed, I saw my first eagles and moose, heard my first loon calling in the night, and ate breakfast to the soundtrack of American bitterns and spring peepers croaking along the shoreline. Unbelievably, we filled our drinking water containers from mountain streams and drank the water untreated. That experience of seeing, hearing, and smelling the beauty of God's creation in a new and fresh way was life changing, helping to form my faith and understanding of the goodness of God and of the wonder of his creativity.

A few years ago, my teaching job required me to live in college housing in the center of town. For several years we rented out our home on a wooded hillside property a half dozen miles away. This meant putting our garden and fruit trees in somebody else's care, along with our meadows and woods, as well as the house itself. Many readers of this book may have had a similar experience of renting out a home and property or leaving it in the care of house-sitters. Or perhaps you have been on the other end, as the one doing the renting or house-sitting. Maybe beloved pets have been involved. When my wife and I put our home and property in the care of tenants, we had two hopes and goals. One was that our house would be a blessing to those who lived there, many of whom we got to know over their time as our tenants. This was especially true in our sixth and final year renting out the house, when our tenants were our oldest son and his wife. At the same time, though, we also wanted our house and property to be well taken care of. That was our second hope. We had lived in that home for fifteen years and invested time and energy into caring for it. It sat on land we were fond of, where I had planted fruit trees and berry bushes and nurtured the garden soil. Furthermore, we planned to return there after a few years living away.

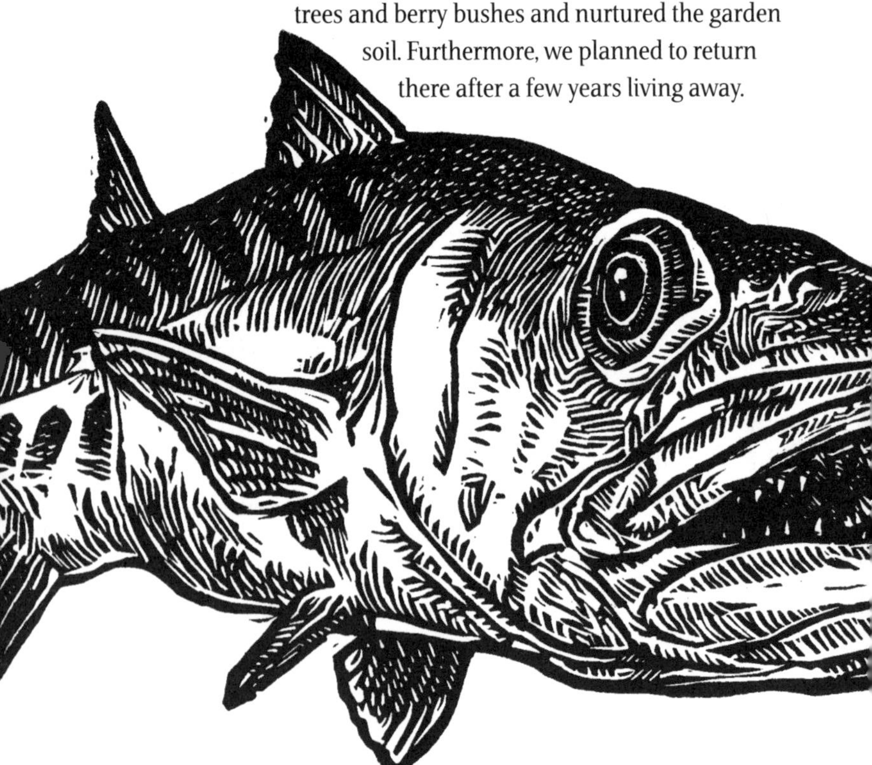

As those who have been in this situation know, even if *you* really love your home, and *your* desire is for it to be well cared for, the moment you give somebody else the keys, you have subjected the house to the actions of the house-sitter. You have voluntarily given to another person some of your authority, and their behavior will impact your house and property. You have allowed the possibility it will be loved, but also the possibility that it will be poorly treated. If your house-sitters throw wild parties, leave food around, play catch inside with a baseball, or spill drinks on the floor without cleaning up, your house is going to bear the consequences. It would not be the house's fault if it suffers from decay and corruption, or if it smells like mice and stale beer. When you subject the house to the authority of the house-sitter, the house will suffer if that house-sitter behaves badly and not in keeping with your plans. The same might could also be said for lending out your car.

This is the story of creation and the fall, told in Genesis 1–3, which Paul refers to in Romans 8. As we explored in the previous section, God gave to his image-bearing humans the vocation of creation-care: to *take care of* (or *keep*) his created world in a way that would bring about its blessing and flourishing. With that responsibility came authority; God entrusted his beloved creation to *us*. What an amazing thought! However, for God to give us the freedom to care *well* for his created world also meant giving us the freedom to destroy or exploit it. This is true of every aspect of our gift of

free will, isn't it? Freedom to love and obey God means freedom
to reject and disobey God. By necessity, the wonderful gift of
freedom to love our spouses and children implies a freedom *not*
to do so. The freedom to use our spiritual gifts and talents for
God's glory is the same freedom allowing us to use them for our
own aggrandizement, or to not use them at all. So it is with the
freedom and responsibility to care for creation. This is precisely
the situation Paul describes in Romans 8:19–21:

> For the creation waits in eager expectation for the children
> of God to be revealed. For the creation was subjected to
> frustration, not by its own choice, but by the will of the
> one who subjected it, in hope that the creation itself will be
> liberated from its bondage to decay and brought into the
> freedom and glory of the children of God.

Paul writes of creation having been "subjected to frustration."
This is an echo of Genesis 1–3. To say that God gave humans
authority over creation is another way of saying God subjected
creation to the authority of humans. The rebellion described in
Genesis 3 leads to frustration for all of creation. As Paul goes on
to say, creation is in "bondage to decay."

I wrote earlier about the naming of the animals in Genesis 2,
and about the sort of intimacy humankind was intended to have
not only with God and with each other but also with creation.
When I wrote that, I was thinking also about the sad results of the
fall and how the breaking of our intimacy with God also corre-
sponded with the breaking of our human relationships and the

breaking of our relationships with the rest of creation. In the next chapter, Genesis 4, we read of human killing human. But even before that, at the end Genesis 3, directly as a result of human sin some of the very animals that Adam had named are killed in order to make skins for the man and woman. We also read that the land itself is now more hostile to human presence, resisting cultivation and growing thorns instead of the desired fruits.

The seriousness of that consequence suggests that human relationships with the rest of creation were different and far more intimate before the fall than after. In any case, Paul's imagery of bondage in Romans 8 is reminiscent of Israel's enslavements to Egypt and Babylon, and more generally of human bondage to sin. Creation suffers from the results of our sin. Both Genesis 1 and John 1 tell us that everything that exists was created by God. Thus all of nature is part of the creation: the ancient giant sequoias and the saguaros of the Senora Desert; the thirteen-foot-tall polar bears of the Arctic and the little lizards

that crawl in the deserts; the soil, water, and air; the prairies and the mountains; every living thing that has ever walked the earth, put down roots, swum in the oceans, or flown in the skies; as well as even the inanimate objects that surrounded them which, as Psalm 148 suggests, all praise God in some mysterious way. All of it, Paul writes, "has been groaning as in the pains of childbirth right up to the present time" (Rom. 8:22).

And here is an interesting thing about Romans 8: Paul tells us that God's plan for restoration and resurrection is not only for humankind; his letter speaks of God's ultimate plan being the restoration of *all* creation, including liberation from its bondage. The creation waits eagerly for that time, even as we do. And if our prayer is for God's kingdom to come and his will to be done on earth as in heaven, then our lives ought to reflect those principles of God's kingdom in the ways we care for creation today.

This leads us to another interesting observation about this passage that relates to both glory and groaning. Romans 8 reveals an interesting progression. Verse 17 speaks of those who follow Christ in his sufferings also sharing in his glory. Verses 17–21 then speak of creation sharing in *our* glory. So the interesting progression is that Christ shares with us his glory, and we then will share that glory with the rest of creation. To rephrase this slightly, God's glory passes down through Christ to Christ's followers and then from those followers on to the rest of creation when we (human image-bearers of God) finally begin to live in the new kingdom and to care for creation in the way we were intended to. This progression reminds us that Christ has authority over us, and has given to us an authority over creation.

But that day has not happened yet. We are still in the time of waiting: the time of groaning. Biblically speaking, we are in a time of lament. And when it comes to groaning, Romans 8 shows a progression in the opposite direction: verse 22 speaks of creation groaning, and then verse 23 speaks of God's human children—"we ourselves, who have the firstfruits of the Spirit"—joining in with creation's groaning "as we wait eagerly for our adoption to sonship, the redemption of our bodies." Finally, verse 26 completes that progression as "the Spirit himself intercedes for us through wordless groans." So as we lament with and for a suffering creation, the Holy Spirit groans with us—a picture reminiscent of that revealed through the prophet Jeremiah centuries earlier of God and then Jeremiah lamenting at the desolation of creation caused by the wickedness of the Israelites.

This all leads us back to the subject of attentiveness. A final reason to be attentive to creation is that we might actually groan with and for the suffering of the world. And as we do so, through our attentiveness we can see how we might also take part in God's kingdom work of healing those sin-caused wounds as we await the final day when God will fully bring about that healing. We do this work knowing that until the day of Christ's return, all human efforts will fall short: we will struggle and at times fail; we will face opposition and disappointment. But isn't this true of all endeavors to live out the principles of God's kingdom? We could say the same about our efforts to serve the church and make disciples, or our efforts to love and care for our friends, parents, spouses, and children. In his book *Into the Heart of Romans,* N.T. Wright speaks of the problem Paul is addressing in Romans 8 as a "crises of the whole cosmos, within which human beings were from the start designed to play a vital role." He goes on to elaborate on Paul's message, "that the whole creation will be rescued from its groaning, sorrow and chaos when humans are raised

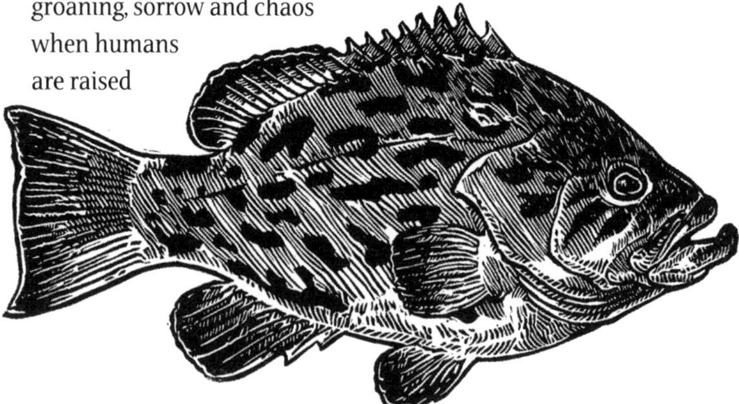

from the dead to take proper charge of it. Salvation is not just God's gift *to* his people, it is God's gift *through* his people."

Wright goes on then to suggest, practically, what we should be doing in light of this, and two of his central conclusions are that we ought to be both groaning *with* creation and caring *for* creation. This excerpts below from this passage are rather long, but worth quoting:

> So, if the "glory" in verses 18 to 21 refers to the wise rule of God's image-bearing people over creation, the primary way that comes to expression in the present time is by prayer, particularly by lament. Particularly if you're a minister of the gospel, but also for every Christian sooner or later, there will be times when, as Paul says here, things will be so bad that you won't even know what to pray for. That does not mean you've gone off the rails somewhere.... It could well mean that you are called to share, in the spirit, the agony of Jesus in Gethsemane and on the cross itself, as part of the ongoing, spirit-led application of God's strange work of taking the pain and sorrow of the world upon himself.... This vocation will come for us whether were ready or not. You see, this passage [Romans 8:16–27] is all about being co-glorified with the Messiah—which sounds wonderful, until we recall that, for Jesus, glorification meant being betrayed, denied, vilified, whipped raw and hung up to die. . . . to say it again, standing at the place of pain isn't just something nasty to get through. It is a vital part of the

means by which God is working out, in the present time, his glorious rescuing purposes for his world. Learning to lament is a non-negotiable part of becoming the people through whom God is accomplishing his saving plan for the whole creation. (138, 141–2)

We must be attentive to creation's groans in order both that we may groan *with* creation (even as the Holy Spirit is attentive to us and groans with us) and also that we might see what the wounds are and do what is in us for the healing of those wounds and the proper care of creation we were called to.

In the end, when Deborah and I moved back to our house, we found that it had (as we hoped) been for the most part well cared for. One set of renters (with our permission) even did some interior painting for us. They kept the lawn mowed and continued to be vigilant about the mice that constantly did their best to invade the house. And we were told that the house and surrounding land was a wonderful blessing to the stewards we left in charge of it.

Sadly, though, the garden and trails through our woods did not fare as well. The tenants, all working full-time jobs, didn't have a lot of time to garden or care for the woodlands and meadows. Thus, when we returned after six years, we found our vegetable plots overrun by deeply rooted weeds, and our fields and the trails through the woods overgrown by a host of invasive and harmful plants. In the years we have been back, we have been working hard to remove the most harmful of those plants and doing our best to replace them with native plants that are beneficial to the local birds, wildlife, and pollinators. Like all struggles against the impacts of sin on creation including humankind, it is a battle that will last until we no longer own the property or until Christ returns. Whichever comes first.

Weeding Peas

Despite persistent efforts to restrain
the hated *quickweed,* it pops up overnight
among the peas. So I must fight the fight
against the blight. And though an effort vain,
this long campaign, I join in Adam's toil
of sweat and pain against the weed and thorn
that plague the gardens of those later born
of Eve. To harvest food, I purge the soil
of *hairy galinsoga* and its kind.

Despairing, losing ground, I curse and swear
at yellow-blossomed plants. I tug and tear,
not seeing all my tender peas entwined
around them, 'til the plants I raised from seeds
pop from the soil entangled with the weeds.

RESTORING WATERSHEDS

As our canoe drifts downstream on Maine's Androscoggin
River, with an occasional dip of our paddles in the water
to keep it straight, a great blue heron spreads its wings
and lifts slowly off the riverbank where moments
earlier it had stood quietly beneath the cedars. With
a cumbersome flapping of wings, it disappears
around the bend. It's a scene I've seen countless
times before, along with kingfishers diving from
shoreline branches in a blur of blue and
white, white-breasted osprey hovering
high in the sky before plunging straight
downward and hitting water talons first
with a much more explosive splash, and
bald eagles soaring overhead with a seeming majesty that
belies their scavenger nature. I still delight whenever I see a
blue heron along a riverbank, even as I feel guilty
for having spooked it from its hunting spot. "I'm
not a threat," I sometimes say aloud. "I'm not
here to eat you." But they never listen. And I don't
blame them. If I were a non-human creature sharing this world
with humans, I think I would also make myself scarce when
humans appeared. For a long time, I thought the color-inspired
name of this prehistoric-looking wading bird—simultaneously
graceful and gangly, awkward and awe-inspiring—was an
exaggeration. To my eyes, it seemed more gray than blue, at least

on the underside that I most often viewed as it flew off. Then one day I finally caught a glimpse of its gorgeous bright blue wing feathers. Such extravagant beauty! The bird is equally at home catching brook trout, shiners, smelt, whitefish, leopard frogs, and northern water snakes along a cold Maine river as it is snatching up baby alligators on a Florida wetland.

I have paddled the Androscoggin from Gilead to West Paris in June when a huge hatch of fluttering white caddisflies was rising off the river and filling the air like a snowsquall moving backward through time. The air can be so thick with them that you can't open your mouth to talk without swallowing a mouthful. Though I don't "love" caddisflies the way I "love" ice cream or dark chocolate, I do have a great appreciation for these benthic macroinvertebrate creatures that (like amphibians) have both a juvenile aquatic stage and an adult air-breathing stage of their life cycle. Like aquatic versions of moths, many caddisflies (a generic name for the more than fourteen thousand species of the order *Trichoptera*) spin silk. But unlike terrestrial *lepidoptera* that only spin cocoons when they are ready to metamorphize from caterpillar to moth or butterfly, these silk-spinning caddisflies actually make their own mobile homes for self-protection, using their silk to glue together into a hard protective shell whatever materials they have available on the stream bottom. Their heads and legs will stick out the front as they walk along the stream bottom foraging, but at the sight of danger they quickly disappear back inside like turtles into shells. They are architects. The New England species I am most familiar with usually do their homebuilding with organic matter found on the stream or lake bottom. However, in some rivers that have less bio matter— rivers through drier climates of the American southwest, for example— they will build homes out of tiny rocks. If the pebbles are colorful enough, then the caddisflies are not only building homes; they are custom-making beautiful pieces of unique jewelry. I have found such caddisflies in colorful casings in high alpine rivers of New Mexico's Gila National Forest. Now, as we drift down the Andro-scoggin River, I gaze at a sky full of their fluttering adult forms, equally full of wonder.

The image of the scene stays with me. I will remember it when I am on a different small tributary river an hour to the north and again find myself in the middle of a caddisfly blizzard. I will think about the scene more than a year later as I drive four hours east from my home in Vermont to spend a week in Maine.

The trip will begin with two-and-a-half days of fishing with my brother Ted, followed by a three-night stay at the Appalachian Mountain Club's Little Lyford Lodge, where I will work on a magazine story about the West Branch of the Pleasant River. As the date of the trip got close, Ted and I had kept an eye on the weather and pondered which of many western Maine rivers, ponds, lakes, or streams we might fish together. One of the leading candidates is the Androscoggin.

As discussed in the previous chapter, forty years earlier we would not have considered the idea of canoeing or fishing the polluted Androscoggin. Not even for a second. But a little over fifty years ago, Maine senator Edmund "Ed" Muskie had seen and smelled the groaning of creation in the form of the Androscoggin River that flowed through his hometown of Rumford, Maine. The terrible pollution in the Androscoggin prompted him to draft the 1972 Clean Water Act. That Ohio's Cayahoga River had famously caught on fire at least a dozen times certainly helped gain support for Muskie's cause. As a result of that Clean Water Act, the Androscoggin is once again a beautiful river in which many species of native fish thrive, along with frogs, snakes, bald eagles, osprey, and great blue herons.

The much smaller West Branch of the Pleasant River three hours to the northeast, where I will go after my time with my brother, is another river that is healthier today than it was a few decades ago. Although it never suffered from the same sewage and paper mill effluent of the Androscoggin, and a remnant population of clean-water-loving brook trout still inhabited many stretches of the river and its headwaters, the river had been much degraded by a combination of clearcutting, careless road building, and the development and industry associated with the Katadhin Iron Works of the late nineteenth century. Among the main culprits were the countless metal culverts used to make hastily constructed lumber roads over streams. These fragmented the rivers, cutting off trout in the main stem from their spawning habitat in smaller tributaries, and caused the river to flow warmer and muddier than it should have. But over the past couple decades, combined efforts of conservation groups like Trout Unlimited working with the Appalachian Mountain Club, which purchased and now manages the property, the culverts have slowly been removed and replaced with natural stream crossings. Some of the lumber roads have been permanently retired, and ongoing lumbering is now done in a much more sustainable and less damaging way.

So when I stand on the bank of the West Pleasant with my friends Ira, Linda, Bryce, and Kenny, none of whom had much experience fly fishing, I am delighted to find an abundant population of wild native brook trout—a fish in the char genus closely related to Alaska's Dolly Varden. Decorated with round golden gems on a dark olive canvas, along with little red cherries haloed with a faint but beautiful circle of sky blue (that is easy to miss at a quick glance but hard to ignore once seen), and fins tinted with red and fringed in white, they are the only fish I have seen that match the beauty of a Dolly Varden. Indeed, a male brook trout in the fall has a blood-red belly and lower jaw every bit as bright and ostentatious as a Dolly. They can also be fierce predators. Though they must watch out for otters and osprey as well as kingfisher, loon, and mink, among

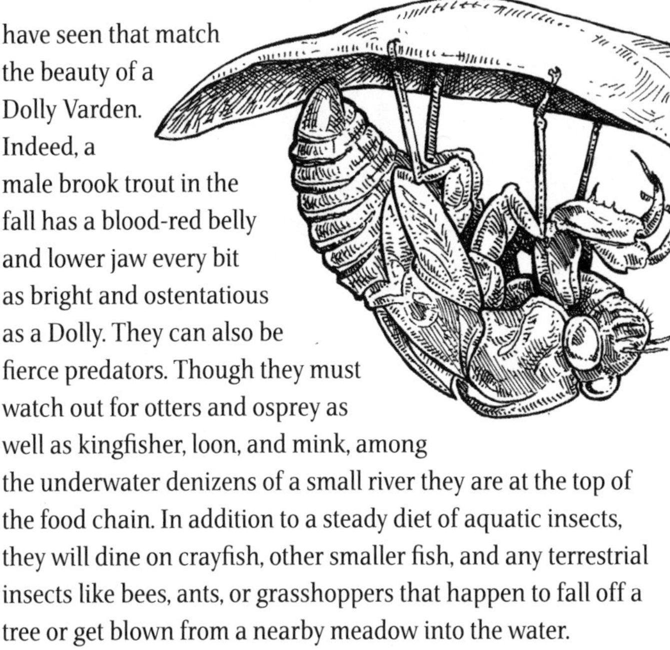

the underwater denizens of a small river they are at the top of the food chain. In addition to a steady diet of aquatic insects, they will dine on crayfish, other smaller fish, and any terrestrial insects like bees, ants, or grasshoppers that happen to fall off a tree or get blown from a nearby meadow into the water.

So I start my friends fishing with a mix of imitation caddisflies floated down the surface, and little streamer flies glided through the water like a swimming fish. I am delighted when Linda manages to catch her first little wild brook trout just minutes into our afternoon outing. She brings it to shore where I carefully hold it underwater for her to admire before releasing it. Soon, Kenny is getting trout to rise to the surface to snatch his imitation caddis. And before twenty-four hours have passed, all have had opportunities to admire some colorful trout. All the while, I delight in how abundant the fish are in the river, with

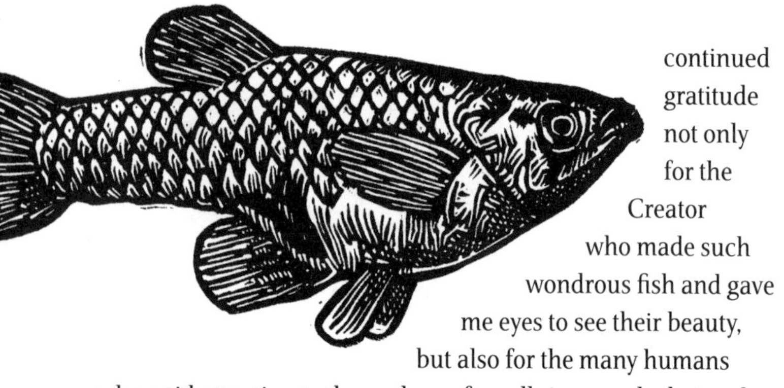

continued gratitude not only for the Creator who made such wondrous fish and gave me eyes to see their beauty, but also for the many humans who paid attention to the ecology of small rivers and what makes them flourish, and who worked so hard to restore the West Branch of the Pleasant to a flourishing state.

And that brings me finally back to Florida and to my recent visit to some of the waters that have inspired Matt Clark and his family, and filled them with awe, wonder, and delight as they have practiced attentiveness in a very different setting. Earlier I spoke of a morning spent at a public city park called the Orlando Wetlands. When I first looked across the water at the grove of cypress trees and the myriad birds moving about their branches, it was impossible for my eyes not to be drawn to the large flock of roseate spoonbills. From a distance, they were so large, abundant, and colorful, with their bright pink bodies and rose-red shoulders, that the bird-filled trees might have felt at home among flaming maples on a Vermont autumn hillside. Later, when we walked the boardwalk out over the water and saw the spoonbills up close, I admired not only their coloring but also their most famous feature. It turns out that a spoon is not only a great shape for eating soup, cereal, and ice cream, but also for scooping crustaceans and mollusks out of the sediment. Like another of Florida's famously colored birds, the pink flamingos of the Everglades, spoonbills were hunted almost to extinction in the eighteen and nineteenth centuries so that their feathers could decorate hats.

There was something I didn't mention earlier about this amazing habitat where we saw not only spoonbills, but a variety of wading and water birds including glossy ibis, wood storks, sandhill cranes, great egrets, cattle egrets, great blue herons, black-bellied whistling ducks, common gallinules, common morehens, anhingas, and also one little blue heron and one green heron. Describing the beauty in the unique body and wing shapes, patterns, coloration, or calls of any one of these alone could fill paragraphs. And then we could move on to the other birds and creatures found there: osprey, red-shouldered hawks, and also alligators and numerous varieties of fish and turtles swimming beneath the boardwalk. What I didn't say was that this whole wetland, with all its amazing bird and wildlife habitat, was built as a sewage treatment facility.

The history goes back to two problems that might be called "environmental" or that Christians might simply refer to as examples of creation groaning. One is that various inhabitants

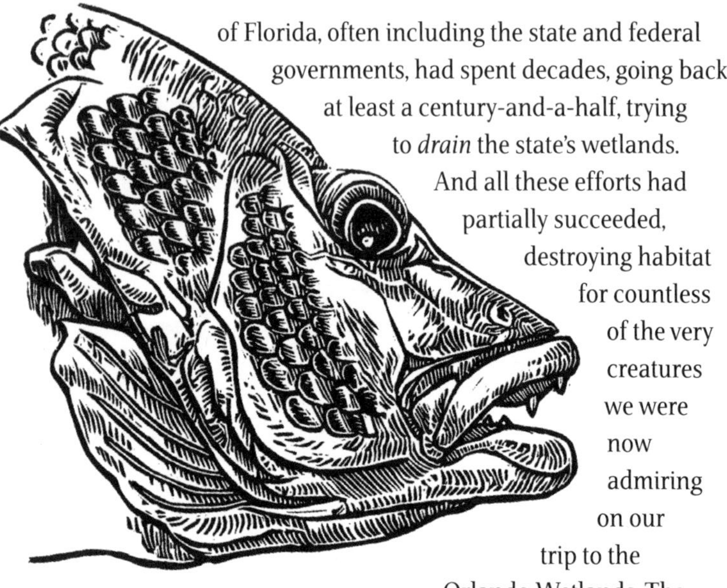

of Florida, often including the state and federal
governments, had spent decades, going back
at least a century-and-a-half, trying
to *drain* the state's wetlands.
And all these efforts had
partially succeeded,
destroying habitat
for countless
of the very
creatures
we were
now
admiring
on our
trip to the
Orlando Wetlands. The
second problem was the need for the city of Orlando to treat
its sewage. The imaginative solution dating back to the 1980s
(the same decade that the Androscoggin River was recovering
from its sewage-related pollution) was for the city to purchase
a 1650-acre ranch in which it dug about thirty interconnected
cells: small ponds separated by berms but with connecting gates
allowing water to drain in parallel series from one to another.
The cells were then planted with several million wetland plants.
In the lowest and largest cell, which is actually a small lake, these
plants included the trees that grew into the cypress dome in
which the numerous birds were roosting. As it turns out, many of

the chemicals in the sewage such as nitrogen and phosphorus, which in large quantities are unhealthy pollutants, are actually nutrients for many plants. As the sewage—or what began as sewage—slowly makes its way through the interconnected cells in a journey that takes almost a month, the plants filter out all those nutrients and all that pollution. By the time the water emerges from the lower end, where it is tested daily by the EPA, it is cleaner than the Saint Johns River into which it flows.

As the iconic 1989 film *Field of Dreams* suggested, if you build it, they will come. And they did. Before long not only birds and fish but also otters, fox, and bobcats began to find their way into the wetlands until it became what it is today: one of the best bird-viewing habitats and sanctuaries in the state of Florida.

A day before that experience, about a two-hour drive northwest of the Orlando Wetland, Deborah and I found ourselves standing on a wooden platform suspended two feet above the Ocklawaha River. We were spending the first full day of our five-night Florida trip with local conservationist Margaret Spontak. Though it was still early May, hot summer air had already arrived. As I mentioned earlier, temperatures had climbed into the upper 90s when our plane landed the previous afternoon. It was only slightly less stifling that morning, and we were happy for any shade or breeze we could find. After a visit to Blue Spring where we found our souls refreshed by the quiet water, followed by lunch with Margaret, our next stop had been the famous Silver Springs on a tributary of the Ocklawaha several miles upriver where we took a one-hour tour on a glass-bottomed boat. We saw a variety of bird life, including

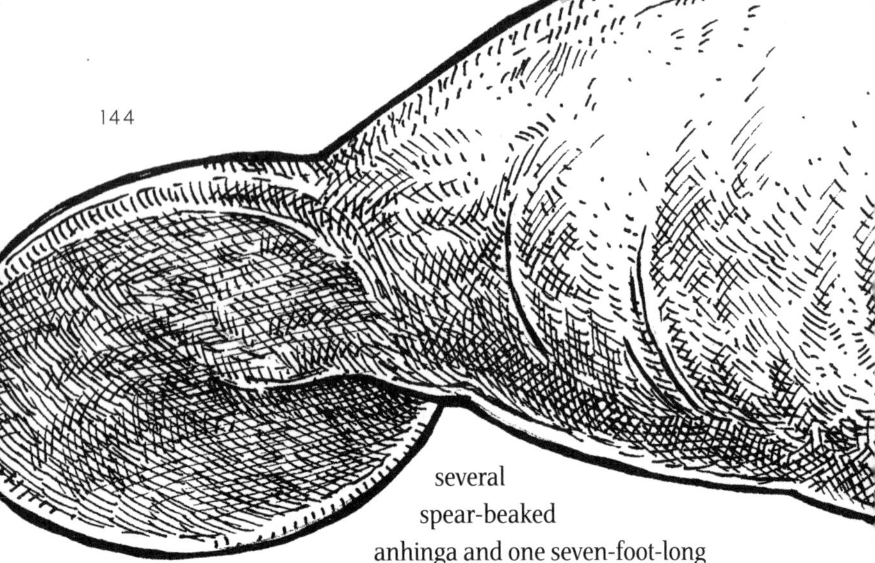

several
spear-beaked
anhinga and one seven-foot-long
alligator resting on a wooded riverbank—a
gator too big to be called a mere "swamp puppy" though not yet
big enough to really impress the boat captain or us, especially
since he was partly up in the trees several dozen yards away with
his business end facing in the opposite direction. We saw no
manatees, however.

Leaving Silver Springs, Margaret had led us down a series of
unpaved wooded backroads to the quiet public fishing access
where we now stood, not because she expected to find manatees,
but because she wanted to show us the fishing platform.
Restoring the Ocklawaha River had been her lifelong passion,
and her vision of a restored waterway involved providing
opportunities for folks to enjoy the river in a variety of different
ways, including fishing. She imagined having a few more similar
fishing access spots constructed—a plan with the benefit of
encouraging more community buy-in to a river restoration

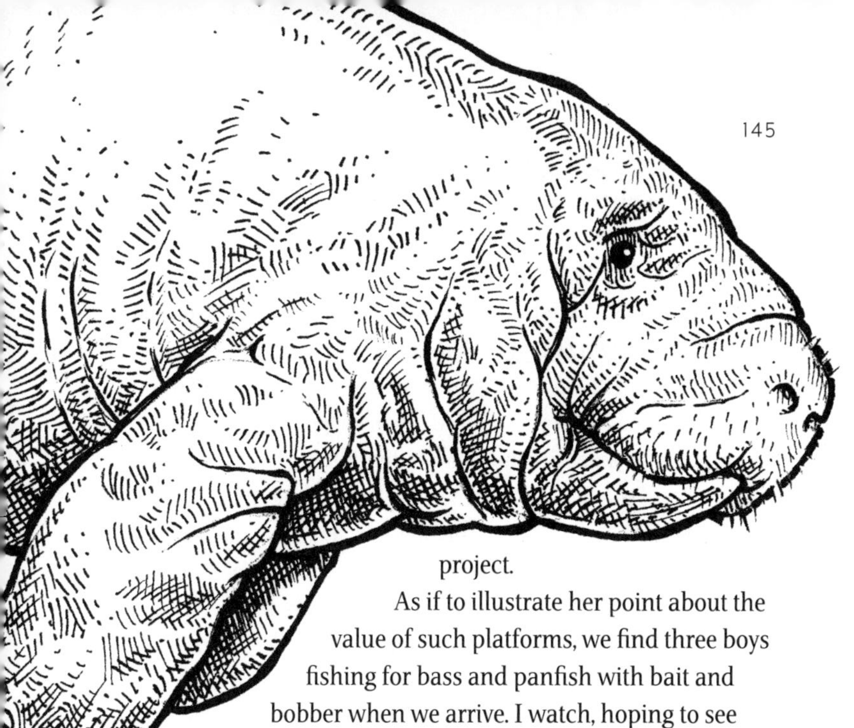

project.

As if to illustrate her point about the value of such platforms, we find three boys fishing for bass and panfish with bait and bobber when we arrive. I watch, hoping to see them catch something, half wishing I could be fishing with them. In addition to largemouth bass and a variety of sunfish, the river's native game fish also include longnose gar, Florida gar, bowfin, and even tarpon.

Beneath and behind the fishing platform, the aquatic vegetation is so thick we can barely see the water below us. In front, where the boys are casting, the river is much deeper. A steady current drifts their bobbers from right to left, requiring them to recast their bait every minute or so. The youngest boy, perhaps tired of the slow fishing, sets his rod down and looks into the water behind them. At once, he excitedly points down into the vegetation, exclaiming aloud that an alligator has just passed beneath the ramp that connects the platform to the shore. The older two boys seem more interested in the fishing than the alligator, but I walk over to investigate. Looking down over the railing in hopes of seeing an alligator up close, I see—or imagine I see—only a slight stirring in the vegetation. Perhaps a large body is moving down there somewhere, but if so the alligator is invisible beneath the grasses and lily pads, presumably waiting in ambush for a passing meal. My attention turns from the alligator and the fishing to some splashing in the river some forty or fifty yards downstream of the platform. Looking more closely, I spot some big submerged bodies roiling the water. When a pair of wide flat flukes lifts slowly up into the air, I realize what they are. Instantly, I become the one shouting excitedly. "Manatees!"

"Yeah," one of the youths says with a bored shrug, still paying attention to the bobber holding up his bait. "They swam past a few minutes ago."

Deborah and Margaret, however, at once come over to join me and watch. The manatees—there are several of them, though we can't count exactly how many since they are mostly under-water—continue to roll and turn and splash for at least half an hour in what we later learn is a raucous mating dance involving one female and several vying males. We had stumbled by a fortunate accident upon an amazing occurrence that most of our long-time Floridian relatives and acquaintances have never had the good fortune to see. As much as I enjoy fishing, I am too full of wonder and delight at the scene we have stumbled on to regret not having my fishing gear with me. Were it not for the thought of a large alligator hiding in the shallow water below us, I would be tempted to walk along the shore to get a closer view of the manatees. Instead, we enjoy the rare and amazing sighting from a safe and non-threatening distance.

Florida's Ocklawaha River has its headwaters in myriad springs along the western side of the Ocala National Forest and Ocala Wildlife Management Area. From its source in Lake Griffin, it flows seventy-four miles to its confluence with the Saint Johns River, which continues out to Florida's east coast near Jacksonville. At one time, the Ocklawaha flowed freely. Its native species included many anadromous and diadromous fish such as tarpon, sturgeon, and mullet whose life cycles or feeding habits make use of both freshwater and saltwater. Among the river's sources once reachable by fish and mammals migrating from the ocean are many of the famous springs of Florida, which pour out of the ground year-round between 72–74°F.

I mention mammals as well as fish because one of the creatures that once came in large numbers, swimming freely from the ocean up into the Ocklawaha system to make use of these springs, was Florida's iconic West Indian manatees: large aquatic marine herbivores, sometimes known as "sea cows." Although they grow up to thirteen feet long and thirteen hundred pounds, they are different from many marine mammals (such as whales and seals, which are known for the blubber) in that they have low body fat. As a result of that low fat and their slow metabolism, they cannot tolerate cold water; they get hypothermic if they stay in water below 68°, and they die in water below 60°. So in the winter when the rivers and coastal waters get cold, they seek out the warm springs. Silver Springs is one of those places. The exact count and locations of the springs in the Silver Springs group changes periodically since individual springs occasionally collapse and then underground water pressure erupts elsewhere to form a new one. But according to the Saint Johns River Water Management District there are currently thirty, with a combined output of about 550 million gallons of water per day—enough water to form an entire river.

Continuing down into the Ocklawaha and from there to the Saint Johns, the water coming out of Silver Springs ought to flow freely to the ocean. It does not. Although ongoing studies between 1826 and 1911 all suggested that a cross-Florida barge canal was a bad idea—economically as well as ecologically—the promise of saving money by making an easier trade route from the Atlantic to the Gulf of Mexico was too tempting for some to pass up (See the "History of the Cross Florida Greenway," at www.floridastateparks.org/learn/history-cross-florida-greenway.). After years of starts and stops, ground-breaking began in 1964. One of the major aspects of the project was building a large dam on the Ocklawaha, forming Ocklawaha Lake. In place of the old river channel was a new straight canal and lock system connecting the lake back to the Saint Johns River.

Although the dam was built, the cross-Florida canal was never completed. The environmental costs, including the impact of Florida's important aquifer and to rivers such as the Ocklawaha, along with the tremendous construction costs, far outweighed any benefit. By the time the project was halted in 1971, however, the damage had been done: the Ocklawaha no longer flowed freely to the ocean. Though a few manatees each year manage to navigate through the lock system and migrate up the Ocklawaha to their historic winter habitats, many die in the attempt. Most just turn back at lock. Of course, the migration route of spawning fish was also blocked.

Our guide Margaret—president of the Great Florida Riverway Trust and founder of the Reunite the Rivers coalition—is one of those who heard the groaning of creation, paid attention to it, and let her lament turn into the work of creation care and healing. One of her lifelong efforts has been to see the dam on the Ocklawaha removed so that Silver Springs and the Ocklawaha River can connect once more to the Saint Johns and the Atlantic Ocean as a free-flowing river where manatees as well as sturgeon, mullet, and tarpon can freely migrate, restoring an ecosystem vital to many other species of birds and wildlife.

Standing with her, I am caught up in the beauty of the place and the creatures that live here, thrilled that I was able to see some of the few manatees who succeeded in finding their way up here. My hope is also lifted by the thought that many more humans might find wonder and delight in creation in a restored waterway, whether through picnicking, paddling, birdwatching and wildlife viewing, or fishing. And that many might turn in delight and praise to the Creator.

Confessional #2

After "Confessional," Mark Heard (1951–1992)

You wrote of windy loneliness,
hearing nothing, seeing shadows.
I have been there too, in the largeness
of this outdoor room. Felt the sting
of a bitter breeze. The sharper solitary
pain.

I've seen berries drape the ground,
sockeye sprawled eyeless on the shore,
a miniature birch bent like a scarred
finger, while a sow bear grows fat
on salmon eggs, and seagulls feast
on the spoils.

You wrote of looking through fog,
waiting for it to lift, catching
a glimpse of something good,
magic, waiting around the corner,
over the hill. I gaze at turquoise
waves, tipped in white.

This is solace for me now.
You have conjured that for me,
like this place. You plucked
the celestial strings. The rest
will wait until the morning
of the resurrection.

Illustration Identification

In the following list, by each page number you will find the common name and the scientific name for the animals and plants illustrated, along with what medium was used for that image. Only one creature in this book is to scale, and that is the fly on page four. The illustrations in this book are made in three ways: pen and ink drawings, etchings, and linocuts. Both etching and linocuts are forms of printmaking. The etchings are first drawn on copper plates which are chemically etched; after this they are printed by means of a press. Linocuts are essentially hand-carved stamps. They are a form of block printing where the drawing is made on a linoleum block and all the white areas are carved out.

PAGE	COMMON NAME	SCIENTIFIC NAME	MEDIUM
cover	Northern Parula	*Setophaga americana*	LINOCUT
cover	Gag Grouper	*Mycteroperca microlepis*	LINOCUT
1	Carolina Chickadee	*Poecile carolinensis*	LINOCUT
2	Nassau Grouper	*Epinephelus striatus*	LINOCUT
4	Housefly	*Musca domestica*	LINOCUT
6	Giant Florida Katydid	*Stilpnochlora couloniana*	LINOCUT
8	Rainbow Trout	*Onorhynchus mykiss*	PEN+INK
	Mayfly	*Ephemeroptera sp.*	PEN+INK
	Double-Crested Cormorant	*Nannopterum auritum*	PEN+INK
13	Apple Snail	*Pomacea paludosa*	PEN+INK
14	Jack-in-the-Pulpit	*Arisaema triphyllum*	LINOCUT
15	Mouse	*Mus musculus*	LINOCUT
16	American Kestrel	*Falco sparverius*	LINOCUT
18	Florida Scrub Jay	*Aphelocoma coerulescens*	LINOCUT
	Prickly Pear Cactus	*Opuntia mesacantha*	LINOCUT
20	House Sparrow	*Passer domesticus*	LINOCUT
22	Squid	*Doryteuthis sp.*	LINOCUT
24	Lavender	*Lavandula sp.*	LINOCUT
25	Paper Wasp	*Vespidae sp.*	LINOCUT
	Rosemary	*Salvia rosmarinus*	LINOCUT
29	Opossum	*Didelphis virginianus*	LINOCUT
31	Trout Lily	*Erythronium americanum*	LINOCUT
	Southern Toad	*Anaxyrus terrestris*	LINOCUT
33	Asian Tiger Mosquito	*Aedes albopictus*	PEN+INK
34	Silver Spotted Skipper	*Epargyreus clarus*	LINOCUT
35	Blanket Flower	*Gaillardia sp.*	LINOCUT
37	Skipper Butterfly	*Hesperiidae sp.*	LINOCUT
	Sweet Potato Flower	*Ipomoea batatas*	LINOCUT

40	**Bottlenose Dolphin**	*Tursiops sp.*	LINOCUT
	Smalltooth Sawfish	*Pristis pectinata*	LINOCUT
42	**Spiny Lobster**	*Panulirus argus*	LINOCUT
43	**Hermit Crab**	*Coenobita clypeatus*	LINOCUT
45	**Blue Orchard Mason Bee**	*Osmia lignaria*	LINOCUT
46	**Tufted Puffin**	*Fratercula cirrhata*	PEN+INK
48	**Rock Hyrax**	*Procavia capensis*	PEN+INK
49	**Nigerian Dwarf Goat**	*Capra aegagrus hircus*	LINOCUT
50	**Brown Anole**	*Anolis sagrei*	LINOCUT
54	**Dolly Varden**	*Salvelinus malma malma*	PEN+INK
56	**Arctic Grayling**	*Thymallus arcticus*	PEN+INK
58	**Brown Bear**	*Ursus arctos*	PEN+INK
60	**Pinfish**	*Lagodon rhomboides*	LINOCUT
62	**Blue Crab**	*Callinectes sapidus*	LINOCUT
64	**River Otter**	*Lontra canadensis*	LINOCUT
66	**King Mackerel**	*Scomberomorus cavalla*	LINOCUT
68	**Lamb**	*Ovis aries*	PEN+INK
70	**Spoonbill**	*Platalea ajaja*	LINOCUT
75	**Alligator**	*Alligator mississippiensis*	LINOCUT
76	**Largemouth Bass**	*Micropterus nigricans*	LINOCUT
79	**Mottled Duck**	*Anas fulvigula*	LINOCUT
80	**Tarpon**	*Megalops atlanticus*	LINOCUT
82	**Herring Gull**	*Larus argentatus*	LINOCUT
84	**Killer Whale**	*Orcinus orca*	PEN+INK
86	**Sea Otter**	*Enhydra lutris*	LINOCUT
87	**Gulf Fritillary**	*Graulis vanillae*	LINOCUT
88	**Caddisflies** (larval form)	*Limnephilidae sp.*	PEN+INK
	Caddisflies (adult form)	*Limnephilidae sp.*	PEN+INK

About the Author and the Artist

MATTHEW DICKERSON published his first book in 1991,
a work of medieval heroic historic fiction. Since then, his published
works have spanned numerous literary categories including
historic fiction, spiritual theology, philosophy and apologetics,
nature writing and ecology, literary exploration, biography, fantasy,
and fly fishing. He is a member of the Chrysostom Society, has
served on the board of directors of the Outdoor Writers Association of America, and has been selected as artist-in-residence for
Glacier National Park, Acadia National Park, and Alaska State
Parks. He has four adult sons and daughters-in-law, and four
grandchildren. With his wife of more than 35 years, he lives on
and seeks to help flourish 62 acres of wooded hillside in Vermont.

MATTHEW CLARK is a teacher at a Christian classical
school in central Florida where he labors valiantly to pass on
his love of creation to both art and science students. Although
he is a Florida native, Matthew spent several post-college years
"trespassing in foreign parts" when he temporarily moved his
growing family to Pennsylvania. He spends his time broadening
his knowledge of the Florida outdoors and in developing his
artwork. In addition to printmaking, Matthew pursues making
artist's books loaded with watercolors and wild drawings.
When not managing an unwieldy number of chickens, dogs,
fish, lizards, snakes and turtles as pets, he and his family can
be found outdoors, crashing through the woods.